pastry

pastry

A Master Class for Everyone, in 150 Photos and 50 Recipes

RICHARD BERTINET

Photos by Jean Cazals

CHRONICLE BOOKS

SAN FRANCISCO

For my beautiful family and chief tasters:
Jo, Jack, Tom, and Lola Maude

First published in the United States of America in 2013 by Chronicle Books LLC.
First published in the United Kingdom in 2012 by Ebury Press, an imprint of
Ebury Publishing, A Random House Group Company.

Library of Congress Cataloging-in-Publication Data available.
ISBN 978-1-4521-1549-8

Manufactured in China

Design: Will Webb
Illustrations: Charlotte Farmer
Prop styling: Jessica Georgiades

10 9 8 7 6 5 4 3 2 1

Chronicle Books LLC
680 Second Street
San Francisco, California 94107
www.chroniclebooks.com

Contents

About the Author

Originally from Brittany, Richard Bertinet trained as a baker from the age of fourteen. Having moved to the United Kingdom in the 1980s, he is now very much an Anglophile.

With twenty years' experience in the kitchen, baking, consulting, and teaching, Richard moved to Bath in 2005 to open the Bertinet Kitchen cookery school. The school attracts people from all over the world to participate in Richard's classes and has been highly praised, including recognition by Ruth Reichl in her television series, *Adventures with Ruth*, in which it was featured as one of the best cookery schools in the world.

As well as instilling passion through his teaching, Richard works as a consultant for major manufacturers developing specialty products throughout the industry.

The Bertinet Bakery started life as a weekly pop-up shop above the cookery school in 2007 but has grown to a much larger affair producing breads and pastries for restaurants, hotels, and food stores in southwestern England, and supplying the bakery's own shops in Bath, with more to come further afield. The bakery's signature sourdough loaf was the winner of the Soil Association's award for Baked Goods in 2010 and 2011.

Richard's first book, *Dough,* received a host of accolades, including the Guild of Food Writers' Jeremy Round Award for Best First Book, the International Association of Culinary Professionals' Cookbook of the Year Award and Julia Child First Book Award, and the James Beard Foundation Award for Baking and Desserts. His second book, *Crust*, was also published to critical acclaim and received a Gourmand World Cookbook Award. His third book, *Cook*, focused on many of the dishes taught at the cookery school. Richard was named the BBC Food Champion of the Year 2010 at the BBC Food and Farming Awards.

Introduction

When I wrote my first book, *Dough*, my aim was to show people that bread making is for everyone and should be fun, not daunting and complicated, which has been the previous experience of many people who come to my classes at the Bertinet Kitchen. Now this book aims to do the same for pastry, because I realize that people are often just as scared of making pastry as bread. There is an idea that some people are just naturally good pastry makers, or that you can only make great pastry if you have cold hands. I don't believe that. Anyone can make fantastic pastry, and I will show you how.

Along the way, I will also talk you through resting and rolling pastry and blind baking. This last technique simply involves baking a pastry crust in the oven without a filling, but the idea seems to cause a lot of confusion. I am constantly asked: Why do you do it? How brown should the pastry be? If you bake it blind, then put in a filling and bake it for another half hour or so, will the pastry burn? How do you stop the pastry from cracking and shrinking in the oven? I will answer all these questions and many more.

One of the reasons that pastry making can seem challenging is that there are so many different names you are likely to come across, from pie pastry to tart-shell or cookie crust, puff, rough puff, pâte brisée, pâte feuilletée, flaky, choux, suet, and hot-water crust. My advice is not to worry about most of these. When you start baking at home, you don't need to master a dozen different kinds of pastry in order to make beautiful pies and tarts to feed the family and impress your friends. Like anything you learn in life, it makes sense to get the basics right and build your confidence, then you can become more adventurous later on. So for this book I have narrowed everything down to just four main categories of pastry, and devoted a chapter to each type.

I call the principal ones simply "salted" and "sweet" because these are the names we used in the bakery where I did my apprenticeship in my native France: *salé* (meaning "salted") for the savory pastry (not because it contains a lot of salt), and *sucrée* (literally "sugared") for the sweet pastry. It was so direct. These are the all-purpose pastries that you can use for any pie or open tart, and they are made using the same method.

As I have said, I try to keep things simple, but in the Salted chapter, I have added a recipe for pork pies made with hot-water crust, which is a pastry used only for making raised pies, the kind you eat cold. I have included it because most people I know love pork pies but think they are tricky to make because traditionally they are "hand-raised," that is, the pastry crust is formed by hand. My recipe is very straightforward and offers a much easier way of making the pies.

The fourth and fifth chapters are about pastries that are both light and airy but have different characteristics and involve two very different techniques. Puff pastry is all about rolling and folding to create layers with air trapped between them so that in the oven this air expands and the pastry literally puffs up (think of millefeuilles and vol-au-vents). By contrast, choux pastry, which is used for things such as profiteroles, involves making a "batter" with the texture of very thick custard. The moisture in the dough creates steam in the heat of the oven and puffs out the pastry, making it quite hollow and airy.

These four pastries are all you need to start to create a wealth of tarts and pies, and even cookies. And I also explain how to present and decorate fruit tarts in the artistic way that makes the displays in French bakeries look so stunning.

Just as *Dough* encouraged everyone to make bread making part of the routine of feeding family and friends, I hope that this book will do the same for pastry, and that by keeping things simple and starting from just four key recipes, you can relax, enjoy yourself, bake with confidence, and perhaps even show off a little bit.

1 The Pastries

In this chapter, I explain how to make four basic pastries, salted, sweet, puff, and choux, which are all you need to make the recipes in chapters 2–5, and to make virtually any other pastry dish you can think of. It's a good idea always to make at least double quantities of salted, sweet, and puff pastry and freeze what you don't use so you will always have some pastry on hand to make a comforting pie or an impressive-looking tart.

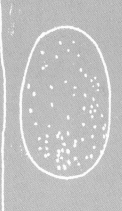

Sizes, Weights, and Measures

Throughout the book, all eggs are US size large and butter is unsalted unless stated otherwise.

Like all bakers and pastry makers, I am a stickler for weighing ingredients because baking is all about being precise and consistent. If you are making a casserole, it really doesn't matter if you use more carrots than parsnips, or a whole bottle of wine rather than half, but if you were to be that loose with your ingredients when you are baking, you would have a disaster on your hands. So when I am making pastry, I weigh everything, including water, because weighing is more accurate than judging the level in a measuring cup. I know it sounds pedantic, but in my classes I encourage people to be as accurate as possible so that they get the best and most consistent results.

I have given the quantity of salt and other ingredients measuring less than 1 tablespoon in teaspoons because the American system of pounds and ounces makes it difficult to weigh out such small quantities.

Ovens

A word about ovens, as I am always being asked what type we use at our bakery and cooking school. Well, we use convection ovens. The heat is more consistent at top and bottom, which helps to give more even baking. That said, if you have a good conventional oven, you will get equally good results.

Some baking books give different temperatures for conventional and convection ovens, but the ethos of this book is to keep everything as clear and unambiguous as possible, so I give only one oven temperature. The reality is that 25 degrees Fahrenheit either way shouldn't make a dramatic difference to your baking. Also, the only way to bake with complete confidence is to get to know your oven. It might give you perfectly uniform heat, or on the other hand it might have hot spots or be slightly hotter or cooler than the dial indicates.

Every oven is different, which makes it difficult to write foolproof baking recipes that will work for every oven in every kitchen. In my classes, I always suggest that the first time you use a recipe, you don't take the baking time as gospel. I have a "five minute rule," which means check every 5 minutes—a tart that bakes in 20 minutes in my oven might need only 15 minutes, or up to 25, in yours. There is no substitute for keeping an eye on whatever you are baking and, if necessary, moving baking sheets and pans higher or lower, or turning them around if you feel one side is coloring more quickly than the other.

After a while, you will get to know the way your oven behaves, and be able to adjust the temperature a little one way or another to suit. Even better, it is worth investing in a good oven thermometer to find out what the temperature actually is in different parts of your oven.

Salted and Sweet Pastry

It is a myth that you need cold hands to make good salted or sweet pastry, but you do need cold butter and a quick, light touch. It is squeezing and overworking that heats up the pastry and makes it greasy and sticky, not the temperature of your hands. In my classes, people are always amazed that I leave the butter in the refrigerator until I am ready to use it, as most pastry recipes call for softened butter. Then, unless you have planned ahead, the temptation is to put the butter into the microwave to soften it quickly, and it melts and turns oily, which makes your pastry even more likely to be greasy. The key is to keep the butter very cold but still soft and pliable, and I will show you how in the method beginning on page 18.

Although you can mix pastry by machine, doing it by hand is such a quick and easy process that I suggest you do it that way, at least at first if you are new to making pastry. Even if you move on to using a machine later, you will get the feel of what you are looking for in terms of texture, and be more in control of the machine. Besides, you still need to finish the dough off by hand once it is mixed.

There was a time when pastry recipes always began by telling you to sift the flour, but nowadays there is usually no need to because the modern milling process sifts the flour so many times that it will flow quite freely and have no lumps. The only time I sift flour is when making choux pastry, because this helps incorporate it more swiftly and smoothly into the mixture of boiling water and butter. (For the same reason, I would also sift the flour when making a sponge cake, as the flour needs to be quickly folded in at the last minute.)

Once you are comfortable with making salted and sweet pastry, you can vary the flavors in any number of ways, perhaps replacing some of the all-purpose flour with whole-wheat or semolina flour, adding caraway seeds, chocolate, or the zest and juice of a lemon. For some of the recipes, I have suggested using a particular one of these flavored pastries, but you can experiment as much as you like.

Salted pastry

This recipe makes about 15 ounces of pastry dough, and each of the recipes in the Salted chapter uses 1 recipe of it. This is enough dough for any of the following pan sizes:

- 24 tartlets made in 12-hole tartlet pans
- 8 individual tarts made in 4-inch removable-bottomed pans (¾ inch deep)
- 1 large tart made in a 10¼-inch removable-bottomed pan or ring (1½ inches deep)

These sizes are what I use in my kitchen, but don't worry if your pans or rings are slightly different. And naturally, you can use whatever shape of pan or ring you like: just keep an eye on your tarts and pies while they bake, as you might need to adjust the time in the oven (see page 13). If you don't need all the pastry, you can freeze what is left (see page 63).

1 egg	
8.9 ounces all-purpose flour	*250 g*
1 teaspoon sea salt	
4.4 ounces butter, straight from the refrigerator	*125 g*
1.2 ounces cold water	*35 g*

Salted pastry variations

Whole-wheat pastry: Use whole-wheat flour instead of the all-purpose flour.
You might need an extra tablespoon of water.
Spelt pastry: Substitute 4.4 ounces of the all-purpose flour with whole-grain spelt flour.
(If using white spelt flour, substitute all of the all-purpose flour with this.)
Semolina pastry: Substitute 1.7 ounces of the all-purpose flour with semolina flour or polenta, and add a pinch of ground turmeric. *→ 50 g*
Cornish pasty pastry: Use margarine instead of butter (to give the baked pastry the flaky softness that is characteristic of pasties).
Caraway pastry: Add 4 teaspoons caraway seeds to the flour.

Sweet pastry

This recipe makes about 25 ounces of pastry dough, and each of the recipes in the Sweet chapter uses 1 recipe of it. This is enough dough for any of the following pan sizes:

- 36 tartlets made in 12-hole tartlet pans
- 24 slightly larger tartlets made in 3¼-inch removable-bottomed pans or rings (¾ inch deep)
- 12 individual tarts made in 4-inch removable-bottomed pans or rings (¾ inch deep)
- 4 larger tarts, made in 6¼-inch removable-bottomed pans or rings (¾ inch deep)
- 2 large tarts made in 8-inch removable-bottomed pans or rings (1½ inches deep)
- 1 large tart made in a 10¼-inch removable-bottomed pan (1½ inches deep), with enough left over to make smaller tarts of your choice

The recipes in the Sweet chapter use quite a range of pans, as I find that different fruits and toppings lend themselves visually to particular sizes. But remember, the sizes given are just a guide. Feel free to use whatever size or shape of pans and rings you have, and keep checking while the tarts are in the oven, as you might need to adjust the baking time (see page 13). If you don't need all the pastry, you can freeze what is left (see page 63).

2 eggs plus 1 yolk	
12.4 ounces all-purpose flour	350 g
pinch of sea salt	
4.4 ounces butter, straight from the refrigerator	125 g
4.4 ounces sugar	125 g

Sweet pastry variations

Chocolate pastry: Add 0.7 ounce unsweetened cocoa powder with the flour. *20 g*

Almond pastry: Use only 8.9 ounces flour and add 3.5 ounces ground almonds with the flour. *250* *100*

Hazelnut and almond pastry: Use only 9.7 ounces flour and add 1 ounce hazelnuts, 1.7 ounces sliced almonds, and 3.5 ounces ground almonds with the flour.

Pistachio pastry: Use only 8.9 ounces flour and add 3.5 ounces ground pistachios with the flour.

Lemon pastry: Add the grated zest of 1 lemon and the juice of ½ lemon when you add the eggs.

8.9 → 250
9.7 → 275 g
1 → 25
1.7 → 50
3.5 → 100

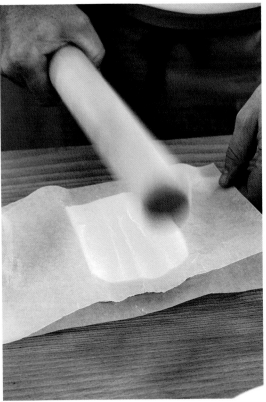

To make the dough by hand

Measure out all your ingredients before you start, and break your egg(s) into a small bowl—there is no need to beat it (them). If making sweet pastry, separate the remaining egg yolk(s). Put the flour and salt into a mixing bowl.

Now for the cold butter. What I do is take it straight from the refrigerator and put it between two pieces of waxed paper or butter wrappers (I always keep butter wrappers to use for this, as well as for greasing pans and rings), then bash it firmly with a rolling pin.

The idea is to soften the butter while still keeping it cold. I end up with a thin, cold slab about ⅜ inch thick that bends like plasticine. Put the whole slab into the bowl of flour—there is no need to chop it up.

Cover the butter well with flour and tear it into large pieces.

Now it's time to flake the flour and butter together—this is where you want a really light touch. With both hands, scoop up the flour-covered butter and flick your thumbs over the surface, pushing away from you, as if you are dealing a deck of cards.

You need just a soft, skimming motion—no pressing or squeezing—and the butter will quickly start to break into smaller pieces. Keep plunging your hands into the bowl, and continue with the light flicking action, making sure all the pieces of butter remain coated with flour so they don't become sticky.

The important thing now is to stop mixing when the shards of butter are the size of your little fingernail. There is an idea that you have to keep rubbing in the butter until the mixture looks like bread crumbs, but you don't need to take it that far. When people come to my classes, I find they can't resist putting their hands back into the bowl to rub it just a little bit more, but if you want a light pastry, it is really important not to overwork it. If the mixture starts to get sticky now, imagine how much worse it will be when you start to add the liquid at the next stage. If you are making sweet pastry, add the sugar at this point, mixing it in evenly.

Pour the egg(s), and the extra yolk if making sweet pastry, into the flour mixture, add the water (salted pastry only), and mix everything together.

You can mix with a spoon, but I prefer to use one of the little plastic scrapers that I use for bread making. Because it is bendy, it's very easy to scrape around the sides of the bowl and pull the mixture into the center until it forms a very rough dough that shouldn't be at all sticky.

While it is still in the bowl, press down on the dough with both thumbs, then turn the dough clockwise a few degrees and press down and turn again. Repeat this a few times.

With the help of your spoon or scraper, turn the pastry onto a work surface.

Work the dough as you did when it was in the bowl: holding the dough with both hands, press down gently with your thumbs, then turn the dough clockwise a few degrees, press down with your thumbs again and turn. Repeat this about four or five times.

Now fold the pastry over itself and press down with your fingertips. Provided the dough isn't sticky, you shouldn't need to flour the surface. But if you do, make sure you give it only a really light dusting, not handfuls, as this extra flour will all go into your pastry and make it heavier.

When you flour your work surface, you need to do this as if you are skipping a stone over water, just tossing out a light spray of flour. (Funny as it seems, people in my classes actually practice this, like a new sport.) You need just enough to create a filmy barrier so that you can glide the pastry around the work surface without it sticking.

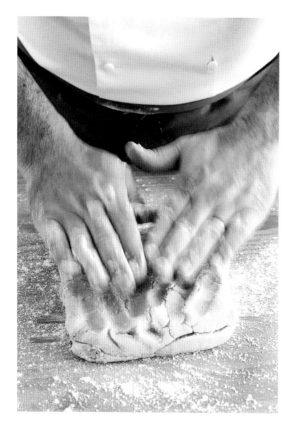 

Repeat the folding and pressing down with your fingertips a couple of times until the dough is like plasticine and looks homogeneous.

Finally, pick up the piece of pastry and tap each side on the work surface to square it off, so that when you come to roll it, you are starting off with a good shape rather than raggedy edges.

To make the dough with a stand mixer

Put the flour and salt into the bowl of the machine. Bash the butter as described in the hand-mixing method, then break it into four or five pieces and add it to the flour. Using the paddle attachment rather than the hook or whisk, mix the ingredients at a slow speed until the pieces of butter are about the size of your little fingernail. You will need to scrape the butter from the paddle a few times as it will stick. If you are making sweet pastry, add the sugar at this point and mix in well. Add the egg(s), and yolk (if making sweet pastry) and water (if making salted pastry), then mix very briefly just until a dough forms. As soon as it does, turn it out onto your work surface with the help of your scraper and follow the hand-mixing method, starting with the second photo on page 23.

To make the dough with a food processor

It is very easy to overwork pastry in a food processor, so be very careful. Put the flour and salt into the bowl of the machine. Cut the cold butter into small dice and add to the bowl. Use the pulse button in short bursts so that the flour just lifts and mixes, lifts and mixes. You don't want to blitz everything into a greasy ball, as that will result in hard, dense pastry. If you are making sweet pastry, add the sugar at this point and mix in well. Add the egg(s), and yolk (if making sweet pastry) and water (if making salted pastry), then pulse briefly just until the pastry dough comes together. Turn it out with the help of your scraper and follow the hand-mixing method, starting with the second photo on page 23.

Resting the pastry

Wrap the pastry in waxed paper, *not* plastic wrap, which will make it sweaty, and rest it in the refrigerator for at least 1 hour, preferably several, or, better still, overnight. The reason you rest pastry is that it helps the gluten in the flour to relax so that the pastry becomes more elastic and easier to roll. It also helps to prevent shrinkage later when it goes in the oven.

If you are really in a hurry to use the pastry, flatten it to about half its thickness with a rolling pin before wrapping it in waxed paper, as this will allow it to chill more quickly. Alternatively, put it into the freezer for 15–30 minutes.

Choosing tart pans and rings

Some of the recipes in this book use 12-hole tartlet pans; others use pans with removable bases, or rings and squares that are simply placed on a baking sheet.

Even if you're using removable-bottomed pans, it is best to put these on top of a baking sheet rather than straight onto the oven rack, partly in case the filling leaks but mainly because it is much easier to move them around and take them out of the oven, especially if you are wearing oven mitts.

It's preferable to use nonstick pans and rings. After baking, I wipe all of mine, whether nonstick or not, with a clean dish towel. I try not to wash them or put them in the dishwasher, and I am careful not to scratch the nonstick ones with anything sharp. Then, before using them, I rub them very lightly with butter (butter wrappers are best for this), or coat them with a little baking spray (again, I do this even if I am using nonstick pans or rings, just in case). If you are going to be baking the next day, you can do this greasing before storing the pans and rings away (that is what I do), so that they are ready to go straightaway.

Rolling out

The secret of a great pie or tart is to get the right balance of pastry and filling so that neither dominates. The more you bake, the more you will get a feeling for this, but for the recipes in this book, I suggest you use a simple guideline. For small tarts and pies up to and including 4 inches in diameter (or the equivalent square or rectangular shape), roll out the pastry 1/16–1/8 inch thick. For larger tarts and pies, roll out the pastry 3/16 inch thick. Remember, if you're not using all of the pastry straightaway, you can divide it up and freeze some of it at this point (see page 63).

Lightly dust your work surface with flour (see page 24), then move the pastry around to coat it. Lightly flour your rolling pin, too. Keeping your fingers on the outer ends of the pin, roll it backward and forward in short, sharp movements without pressing down too hard on the pastry or stretching it.

Keep lifting the pastry up after every two rolls, and move it a quarter turn to get some air underneath it and stop it from sticking to the work surface. Continue rolling until it is the size and thickness required for your recipe, and large enough to leave an overhang when you line your pan or ring.

Roll the pastry around your rolling pin so that you can lift it up without stretching it.

Lining tart pans and rings

To line a 12-hole pan, or 3¼-inch removable-bottomed tartlet pans, use a circular cutter or tumbler to stamp out circles of pastry about 1 inch bigger than the holes or, in the case of individual pans, about 1¼ inches bigger to allow for the depth and leave a little bit of overhang. The 12-hole pans are more common in England, but you could substitute a miniature muffin pan with cavities that hold about 2 ounces each (the same as the individual tartlet pans).

If using individual pans with unusual shapes, such as the leaf ones pictured, place one of them upside down on the pastry and cut around it, again leaving a border of about 1¼ inches. To line larger pans or rings (over 3¼ inches in diameter), make sure you roll out your circle or square of pastry large enough to cover the depth of the pan or ring and leave about 1 inch overhang. If you are using rings, set them on the baking sheet before lining with dough; if using removable-bottomed pans, set them on the baking sheet after lining them with dough so that it is easy to move them in and out of the oven.

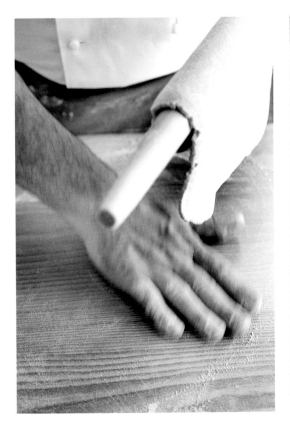 

Lift your rolling pin with the pastry wrapped around it.

Holding the pin at each end, drape the pastry over whatever pan or ring you are using.

Let the pastry fall inside, easing it gently and carefully down into the base and sides without pulling or stretching it.

Leave the pastry overhanging the edges of your pan or ring. If using fluted pans, press the pastry lightly into the shaped sides.

Once your pan is lined, tap it lightly against the work surface to settle in the pastry. If using a ring, just lift up the baking sheet it is sitting on and tap it down. If you are going to blind bake the pastry, see the facing page. Otherwise, put the lined pan or ring in the refrigerator for at least 30 minutes (or in the freezer for 15 minutes). This will help to stop the pastry from cracking, shrinking, and pulling away from the edges when it is later put in the oven.

Remove the pastry crust(s) from the refrigerator. The pastry overhang on large pans can be left in place and removed with a sharp knife just before serving. If you are using small pans, trim the pastry around the edges with a knife *before* filling and baking, as trimming will be tricky to do once the tarts are baked. (Provided the pastry has rested for long enough, it shouldn't shrink.) If the pans are fluted, you might find it easier to carefully tear away the excess with your fingers.

Heating the oven

It sounds obvious, but make sure you turn on your oven in plenty of time so that it is properly hot when you're ready to bake. You don't want your beautifully chilled pastry to sit around getting warm while you wait for the oven to reach the right temperature. One of the secrets of avoiding the dreaded "soggy bottom" and achieving a good, crisp finish to your tarts and pies is to get the heat to the base immediately. As a baker, I always have a hot baking stone, which is actually a piece of granite, in my oven—so every time I switch the oven on, the stone heats up. In my classes, I always suggest people get the same effect at home by using the broiler pan bottom and turning it upside down. Then all you have to do is place the baking sheet holding your pan or pans straight onto it. If you're baking more than will fit on the broiler-pan bottom, you can always put an inverted baking sheet on a separate shelf.

Blind Baking

There is a great deal of confusion about blind baking, and I find it helps to explain that blind baking is not *part* baking, it is *pre*-baking. Baking blind is simply a way of fully baking a pastry crust, large or small, without a filling so that you can use it as you wish—putting in something cold and ready to eat, such as fruit and cream, or adding a liquid filling, such as crème fraîche, eggs, and bacon, that needs to be cooked and set. I know people worry that returning a baked pastry crust to the oven for another 30 minutes or so after it is filled will result in burnt pastry, but once the filling is put in, unless the tarts are very tiny, the temperature in the oven is turned down, and the pastry won't color any more, except around the over-hanging edges, which will be trimmed off anyway.

Why bake blind if you are going to put the crust back in the oven anyway? You do this either because the filling will be set in a shorter time than it takes to fully bake the pastry, or because the filling is very liquid. Think about a mixture for quiche: when you put it in the oven it is quite runny, and even though it will take around the same time to cook as it would for the pastry to bake, the pastry actually has no chance of crisping up with all that wet filling on top. The result: soggy bottom pastry.

I think it helps to understand the principle of what actually happens when you blind bake. You do it in two stages. First, to help the pastry hold its shape when it goes into the oven, you line it with parchment paper filled with ceramic baking weights. Then, once the pastry has begun to dry out and keep its shape, you take it out of the oven, brush it with beaten egg (egg wash), and put it back in the oven to form a hard seal that is fully "waterproof," so the pastry will stay crisp, whatever you put into it.

It's always worth holding on to leftover pastry, even if it's just scraps, because if you are blind baking, these can be used to patch up any broken pastry crusts before they're brushed with egg wash and put back in the oven. Of course, if you have rolled and rested your pastry properly, there won't be any holes or cracks, I hope.

Blind baking removable-bottomed pans and rings

First, prick the base of the pastry all over with a fork. This stops it from rising up when in the oven (even though it will also be held down by ceramic baking weights, it can sometimes manage to lift a little). Unless you are making small tartlets (up to 3¼ inches), don't trim the pastry. Leave it overhanging the edge.

Place a large sheet of parchment paper over the top of the pastry crust, then pour in the ceramic baking weights and spread them out so that they completely cover the base. (Traditionally, dried beans or peas were used for this, and are fine, but the ceramic ones can be kept in a container and used over and over again.) Put the lined pan in the refrigerator for 30 minutes (or the freezer for 15 minutes) to rest and relax.

Preheat the oven to the temperature specified in the recipe. Bake small tarts and pies (4 inches or less) for 15 minutes, and larger ones for 20 minutes. As I mentioned on page 13, in my classes when people ask me how long to bake for, I say, "Five minutes!" Of course they look at me as if I'm crazy, but I explain that I want to get everyone in the habit of keeping an eye on pastry in the oven. If I were to say 20 minutes, in their minds they would just switch off and forget about it for that length of time. But baking times are only a reference, not to be taken as gospel, especially when you are new to baking and not quite sure how your oven behaves. (There is no uniformity where ovens are concerned.) So have a look after 5 minutes, then after another 5 minutes, then . . .

When the base of the pastry has dried out and is lightly golden, remove it from the oven and lift out the parchment paper and weights. Don't worry if the overhanging edges are quite brown, as you will be trimming these away after you have finished baking your tart. Have ready some beaten egg. (I add a pinch of salt, which breaks down the egg and makes it easier to spread with a pastry brush. It also makes the color look darker, so don't worry, this is normal.) Brush this over the inside of the pastry crust to seal it. Hopefully, there will be no cracks or holes, but if there are, don't panic. Just take a tiny scrap of leftover pastry, dip it into your beaten egg, and use your finger to rub it over the crack, as if you were putting filler in a wall. Return the pan to the oven.

 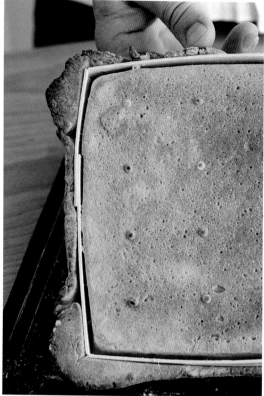

Small crusts need another 8 minutes, and larger ones a further 10 minutes. If you have done a little bit of patching, the extra dough will be so thin that it will bake in this time, and once the pastry crust is filled, no one will ever know. The inside of the pastry will now be quite a dark golden brown and shiny from the egg glaze.

If you turn the tart crust over, the base should also be well browned and crispy.

Blind baking a 12-hole tartlet pan

The easiest way to blind bake a 12-hole pan is simply to put an identical (empty) pan on top, but first grease the base very lightly with butter or a nonstick baking spray. Then put something like an ovenproof dish on top to weigh it down. Bake for the time stated in the recipe, then remove the baking dish and top pan. Brush the inside of the pastry crusts with beaten egg and return to the oven for the time given in the recipe. Alternatively, 12-hole pans can be blind baked in exactly the same way as individual pans and rings, using parchment paper and ceramic baking weights.

Puff pastry

I really hope that when you have the time, you will have a go at making puff pastry, as it is very satisfying. However, I know that it is a long process, and even when you have mastered the technique and gotten into the habit of making it in big batches so that you can keep some in the freezer, there will inevitably be a day when you have none left and no time to make more. Since the whole point of this book is to encourage more people to have a go at baking and enjoy themselves while doing it, I would much rather you used a good, ready-made puff pastry than not bake at all. There are some really good all-butter puff pastries out there, and it is worth keeping a supply in the freezer—hopefully alongside your own homemade pastry.

Puff pastry differs from others in that you make it by constantly rolling and folding the dough so that you create lots of layers or "leaves" with air trapped in between. (The French name for this pastry is *feuilletée*, which means "leafy.") In the heat of the oven, these air pockets expand, so the layers separate and the pastry as a whole puffs up.

The more rolling and folding you do, the more layers you create. Each series of foldings is known as a "turn," and six turns is the ideal. These are easy to achieve in bakeries, where they have an automatic rolling pin called a pastry brake. At home, though, quite a bit of time and effort is involved, as you need to put the pastry back into the refrigerator after each turn so that it is always cold to work with. The first few times you make it, I suggest you do three double turns instead of six single ones, as explained on pages 53–55. In bakeries, this is known as a "double book."

This recipe makes about 1 pound of pastry, but I find it is much easier to make puff pastry in large amounts, so I always suggest making double the quantity, and then putting whatever you don't need into the freezer so you will always have some ready to go (see page 63).

8.9 ounces all-purpose flour	250 g
1 teaspoon sea salt	
3.5 ounces cold water	100 g
juice of ¼ lemon	
7 ounces butter, straight from the refrigerator	200 g

Place the flour and salt in a bowl, and the water in a measuring cup. Squeeze the lemon juice into the water at the last minute. (The juice helps stop the pastry from darkening during the long folding and resting process.)

Gradually add the water and lemon juice, mixing with a scraper or spoon until you have a rough dough.

Turn the dough onto your work surface and knead it by folding it onto itself, then pressing down with your fingertips or the heel of your hand. The important thing is to stop just as it comes together—this will take about 2 minutes—then shape it quickly into a rough ball.

Now you need to make two deep cuts in the shape of a cross on top of the dough, then open it out a little and lift it into a bowl. Cut open a resealable plastic bag, lay it loosely over the top, then rest the dough in the refrigerator or a very cool place for 1 hour.

Very lightly dust your work surface with flour (see page 24) and set your rested dough on it. Gently ease out each of the four corners of the dough.

Then roll out the dough, just until it forms a square of roughly 8 inches. Place your cold butter between two sheets of waxed paper and bash it with a rolling pin (see page 18). You want the butter to be a smaller square shape than your dough, about ¾ inch smaller all round (i.e., roughly 7¼ inches). Lift off the top sheet of waxed paper, then turn the butter over onto the center of the dough so that it is at a 45-degree angle to it (i.e., its straight sides are opposite the corners) and remove the remaining sheet of waxed paper (see photo opposite). Doing this means that you don't touch the butter directly, so you avoid warming it up.

Fold each side of the dough over the butter to enclose it completely in a parcel. This is the crucial part of the process, as you need to make sure there are no gaps where the butter could seep through.

Gently, using your rolling pin, make dents all the way across the parcel to squash the butter a little inside (see photo opposite). Now roll out the pastry lightly and gently, lengthwise only, into a rectangle two to three times longer than its original length. (It's important to do this lightly, because if you press down hard on the dough, you run the risk of the butter warming up and seeping out, and the pastry will become heavy.) Each time you roll, lift the dough a little and move it around slightly to get some air underneath it and help stop it from sticking.

Double book

Turn the dough so a long side of the rectangle is nearest you. Fold in the two ends to meet in the middle, then fold them over again. With your finger, make a dimple in the top of the dough to indicate that this is the first turn. This is an old bakery trick—very handy if you go off and do something else, then forget how many turns you have given the dough. Put the dough on a baking sheet, cover loosely again with the opened-out resealable plastic bag, and leave to rest in the refrigerator for 20–30 minutes.

Lightly flour your work surface and place the rested dough on it with a short end facing you. Roll it again lengthwise, then turn it so that a long side is nearest you and fold as before. This time make two dimples on the top to indicate the second folding, and again rest in the refrigerator for 20–30 minutes. Repeat this rolling and resting process once more. The pastry is now ready to use.

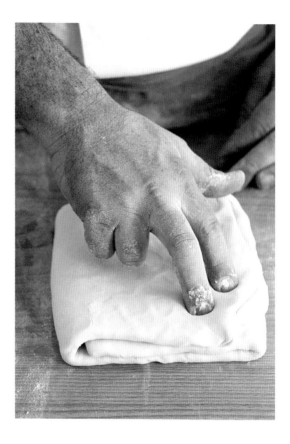

Single turn

Once you are more experienced, you can try doing six single turns rather than the double book described on page 53. Place the pastry with a long edge nearest you, but this time fold in just one side, then fold the other side over the top. With your finger, make a dimple in the top of the dough to remind yourself that this is the first turn. Put the dough on a baking sheet, cover loosely again with the opened-out resealable plastic bag, and leave to rest in the refrigerator for 20–30 minutes.

Lightly flour your work surface and place the rested dough on it with a short end nearest you. Roll it again lengthwise, then turn it so that a long side is nearest you and fold as before. This time make two dimples on the top to indicate the second turn, and again rest it in the refrigerator for 20–30 minutes. Repeat this rolling, folding, and resting process until you have done six turns in all, marking the top of the dough each time with the appropriate number of dimples. The pastry is now ready to use.

Choux pastry

Although this is a type of puffed pastry, it is made using a completely different but very simple technique that involves boiling water and butter in a pan, whisking in the flour, and then beating in the eggs to create a batter the consistency of thick custard. This expands in the oven, leaving a light, airy center.

As I mentioned earlier, while I don't sift flour for making salted or sweet pastry, I *do* sift it when making choux pastry, as it helps to incorporate the flour more quickly and smoothly into the boiling water and butter.

4.3 ounces all-purpose flour	120 g
8 ounces water	225 g
2.1 ounces butter	60 g
½ teaspoon sea salt	
4 eggs	

Have all your ingredients ready before you start. Sift the flour into a mixing bowl. Bring the water, butter, and salt to a boil in a large saucepan.

Pour the flour into the saucepan in a steady stream.

Keep whisking all the time until the mixture clings to the whisk.

Swap the whisk for a wooden spoon and beat well over the heat for 2–3 minutes, until the mixture is glossy and comes away from the sides of the pan. This hard cooking dries off the batter and makes it ready to take the eggs.

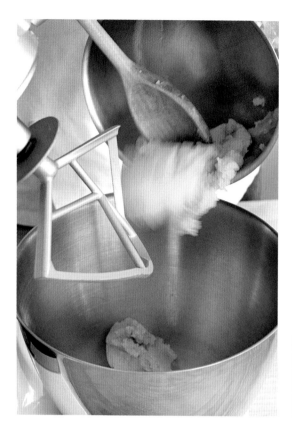 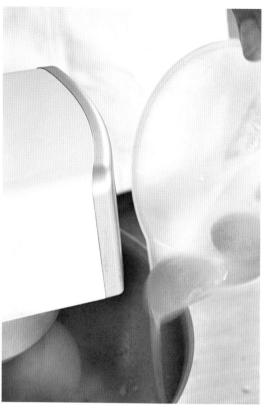

Because the mixture is quite hard to work by hand, I would use a stand mixer, if possible. Beat the mixture with the paddle attachment for 1 minute.

Now start to add the eggs one at a time while keeping the motor running. If you prefer to beat in the eggs by hand, transfer the mixture to a bowl and beat them in one by one with a wooden spoon. Whether mixing by hand or machine, go carefully with the eggs as you might not need them all. You are aiming for a mixture that is smooth and glossy but that will hold its shape for piping. When you reach that point, it is ready to use.

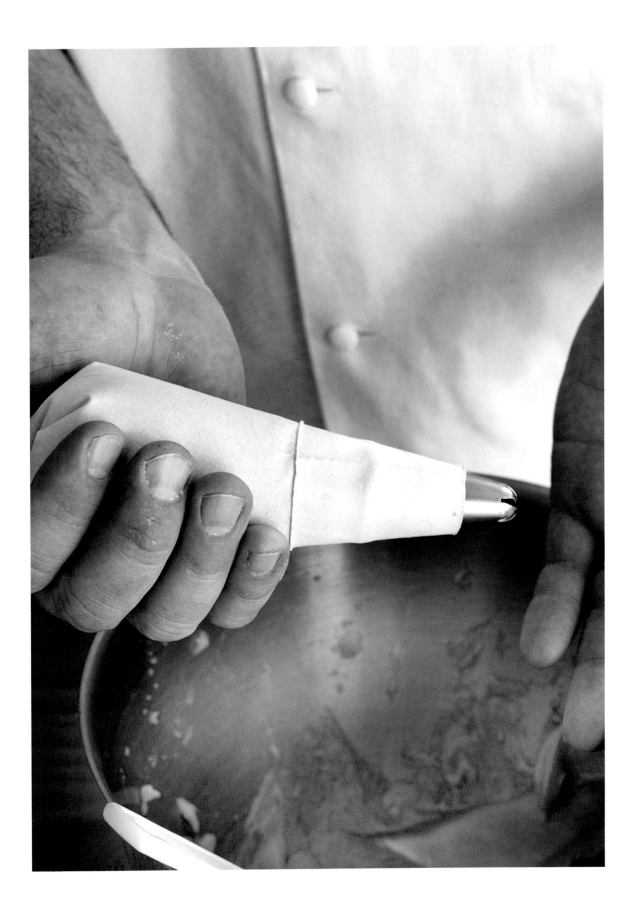

Piping Bags

Of course you can spoon choux batter onto your greased baking sheets in little mounds or strips to make buns or éclairs, but it is much more controllable if you pipe it, and you will need to do this if you want to make the classic choux swans on page 181. Like any other baking skill, piping is about technique and practice—and once you get the hang of it, it is very simple and satisfying to do.

Although you can buy very good disposable piping bags, I prefer the fabric ones because you can get a better grip on them as you pipe. The drawback is that they need to be washed out very carefully with hot soapy water, rinsed, and then hung up to dry somewhere warm, such as near the oven, once they have been used. And they must be completely dry before you use them again. So it is worth investing in several bags in various sizes, especially if you need to have two or three on the go at one time, with different tips, as you do when making the swans. I would suggest buying one large fabric bag, a couple of medium ones, and a small one, so you can adapt to the quantity of batter you need to pipe. The bags have a small hole where the tip goes, and you can cut this to the correct size for the tip you want to use.

You can buy plastic tips, but I like the stainless-steel ones that give a sharper edge to the piping. Again, they come in different sizes, so I would have a set of plain tips in large, medium, and small, and another set of star-shaped tips, again in large, medium, and small.

To fill a piping bag cleanly, turn the bag inside out over one hand and use the other hand to fill it just half full. Pull up the sides of the bag and twist the top so that the mixture is forced down toward the tip.

As I explain on page 182, the way to pipe fluently and stay in control is not to hold the bag in one hand and squeeze with the other, but to squeeze with the same hand that is holding the bag, with your other hand underneath, steadying and guiding as you pipe.

Keeping and freezing pastry

Salted, sweet, and puff pastry will keep for up to 1 week in the refrigerator. However, I always make at least double the quantity of pastry I need and immediately freeze what I am not using. I wrap it first in parchment paper, then put it in a resealable plastic bag and write the date on it. The pastry will keep for about 3 months in the freezer, and you will find that, after defrosting, it is a dream to roll out.

Pastry that has been frozen for about 3 months can discolor a little. If you don't want this to happen, add a drop of lemon juice or vinegar to the water before mixing it into the dough. You won't taste it in the pastry, but it will be enough to keep the dough fresh looking.

If you like, you can roll out your pastry and line your tart pans, then freeze them, stacked inside one another, wrapped loosely in parchment paper inside a resealable plastic bag. Simply defrost before use.

Alternatively, when using salted or sweet pastry, you can blind bake your pastry crusts, remove them from their pans or rings, and keep them in an airtight container at room temperature for 2–3 days before filling.

In the Sweet chapter, the tarts that contain almond cream can usually be frozen in their entirety, or at least up to the point of topping with fruit. Or, they can be baked first, and then frozen—see page 119, together with the instructions in each recipe, for more details. You can also bake cheesecakes (see page 116) in their entirety and then freeze them. When you defrost them, they are ready to eat. Just be aware that the pastry might not be quite as crispy as when it is freshly baked.

I don't recommend freezing choux pastry when it is raw, but once baked, you can put choux buns, éclair shells, and the like on a tray in the freezer and, when they are frozen, transfer them to an airtight container and return to the freezer. Then you can defrost them and fill and/or glaze according to your recipe.

2 Salted

As I mentioned in the introduction, I call this chapter Salted not because the pastry is full of salt, but because this was the generic name for savory pastry that I learnt as an apprentice baker.

The recipes in this chapter are for all the kinds of things I associate with the *traiteur* in France, even though they include very British Cornish pasties, sausage rolls, and pork pies. The *traiteur*'s shop makes the best food to go, and the *traiteur* himself is like a multi-event athlete who has the skills of a baker, pâtissier, butcher, charcutier, and chef without specializing in any one. When I was growing up, it was always a treat to go inside the shop and, from among the many dishes ready to take home, choose a slice of freshly made quiche, a wedge of pie, or a small tart, with a selection of some of the big, colorful salads that would be set out in bowls.

Makes 24

1 recipe Salted Pastry (see page 16)

1 egg, beaten with a pinch of salt, for sealing the pastry

For the base filling

14 ounces (1¾ cups) crème fraîche ⟶ *400 g*

4 extra-large eggs

sea salt and freshly ground black pepper

½ whole nutmeg, grated

Savory tartlets

Yes, the dreaded quiche. In Britain, it is so often associated with bland, soggy slices on the buffet table at parties, but in France it is a staple of the *traiteur*, and the quality of the pastry and the variety of fillings is a matter of pride. Personally, I think a freshly baked quiche, not long out of the oven, with a crisp salad dressed with good vinaigrette, is fantastic. In my classes, to help convert people, we start off by making small tartlets and individual ones rather than big quiches because it is so much easier to roll out the pastry and get it to crisp up well in the oven, eliminating the limp pastry factor that puts off so many people.

The base filling is a mixture of crème fraîche and eggs to which you can add any flavorings or ingredients you like. I use crème fraîche because it is light and has a slight tang, but if you prefer a richer, creamier texture, you can substitute it with heavy cream, or use half crème fraîche and half heavy cream. I have given three of my favorite fillings on page 68, but other ideas include chopped walnuts and Roquefort cheese, or even some slivers of roast chicken plus potatoes and vegetables left over from Sunday lunch. Varying the fillings helps keep the quiches interesting, and is a great idea for parties.

To make things simpler, if you are catering for a number of people, you can blind bake the pastry crusts up to 2–3 days in advance and keep them in an airtight container until you are ready to fill them and pop them into the oven for half an hour or so. I think the tartlets are at their best if you allow them to cool down to room temperature before eating: if they are too hot or too cold, the temperature suppresses the flavor.

I have chosen to make the quiches as tartlets, but they can be made bigger (10¼ inches) if you prefer (see page 16). However, you will need to double the quantity of your chosen filling, and bake them for 30–35 minutes.

(Continued)

Rest the pastry in the refrigerator for at least 1 hour, preferably several, or, better still, overnight (see page 29).

Lightly grease two 12-hole tartlet pans. Dust your work surface with flour, roll out the pastry $1/16$–$1/8$ inch thick, and line the pans (see pages 30–36). Line with parchment paper and ceramic baking weights. Place in the refrigerator to rest for at least 30 minutes (see pages 37–42).

Preheat the oven to 375°F.

Remove the pans from the refrigerator and bake for 15 minutes. Lift out the parchment and weights, brush the pastry with the beaten egg, then bake for another 8 minutes. Set aside.

TO MAKE THE FILLING: Whisk the crème fraîche a little to loosen it, then mix in the eggs with a wooden spoon. (This is a tip I learnt from my days as an apprentice baker in France: using a spoon instead of a whisk prevents overmixing, which can make the filling dense. More restrained mixing helps to lift the filling so it becomes nice and light in the oven.) Season well with the salt and pepper and add the grated nutmeg.

Now you can flavor the base filling as you wish. The three combinations below are my favorites, and each makes enough for 12 tartlets. But you can mix and match and divide or multiply as you like.

Hot variations

Smoked salmon and parsley (or dill): Put 2 cherry tomato halves and some salmon trimmings into each pastry crust, with a little chopped fresh parsley (or dill) on top. Spoon some of the base filling over the top and bake for 25–30 minutes.

Bacon, leek, and reblochon: Gently heat a dry frying pan and, when hot, add 2 chopped slices smoked bacon or 3.5 ounces smoked lardons. When golden, transfer to a paper towel to absorb the excess fat. Boil and slice 2 small potatoes and very finely slice the white part of 1 thin leek. Divide the bacon, potatoes, and leek among the pastry crusts. Spoon some of the base filling over the top, and top with a slice of reblochon (or any cheese you like: Emmentaler, Port Salut, goat cheese, Camembert, Brie, or even Cheddar is fine). Bake for 25–30 minutes.

Mushroom and spinach: Melt a knob of butter in a frying pan, add 6 quartered small button mushrooms, and fry gently for a couple of minutes, until they color a little. Add 5 ounces [140 g] baby spinach and cook quickly until it has wilted. Put the mixture into a sieve and drain off the excess liquid—there should be very little. (You could also use frozen spinach for this; just defrost it quickly and mix it with the sautéed mushrooms.) Divide the mixture among the pastry crusts. Spoon some of the base filling over the top and sprinkle with a little grated Gruyère. Bake for 25–30 minutes.

Cold variations

If you like, you can blind bake the tartlets and keep them in an airtight container until you are ready to fill them with ingredients that need no further cooking—a great idea for parties. Try fillings such as mayonnaise and poached salmon or trout, blanched green beans and a little fresh dill (see photo opposite), smoked salmon and crème fraîche, smoked trout and creamed horseradish, or smoked ham and chutney. Or just experiment!

Makes 24 tartlets

1 recipe Salted or Spelt Pastry (see page 16)

2 tablespoons butter   28 g

large pinch of sea salt

large pinch of sugar

6 onions, thinly sliced

1 garlic clove, crushed

1 bay leaf

1 tablespoon grated Gruyère cheese

24 small thyme sprigs

1 tbsp butter ↝ 14-15 g
1 stick butter ↝ 113 g ↝ 8 tbsp ↝ ½ cup
4 ounces

Onion tartlets

You don't need to blind bake the pastry for these tartlets, as the filling isn't as liquid as the quiche filling on page 67. This means that you can make them up in their entirety and freeze them. Defrost them thoroughly, then bake as normal.

Rest the pastry in the refrigerator for at least 1 hour, preferably several, or, better still, overnight (see page 29).

Preheat the oven to 375°F.

Melt the butter in a heavy-based pan with the salt and sugar. Add the onions, garlic, and bay leaf and cook slowly until the onions are softened and browned a little. Remove the bay leaf.

Lightly grease two 12-hole tartlet pans. Dust your work surface with flour, roll out the pastry ¹⁄₁₆–⅛ inch thick, and line the pans (see pages 30–36). Place in the refrigerator to rest for at least 30 minutes.

Fill the chilled crusts with the onion mixture and top with a pinch of Gruyère and a sprig of thyme. Bake for 18–20 minutes, until the pastry crusts and cheese are nicely browned.

Makes one 10-inch tart

1 recipe Salted Pastry (see page 16)

1 recipe Savory Tartlets base filling (see page 67) plus choice of Hot Variations (see page 68)

Open tart

I sometimes like to make one large, rustic-looking tart, rather than the traditional round quiche. The hand-shaped tart is slid straight onto a preheated inverted broiler-pan bottom or baking sheet at a high heat, so there is no need to chill a dough-lined pan or to blind bake the pastry; the heat of the tray will help to give a nice crisp base. In this case, too, the topping is quite thin, so it will bake quickly.

Preheat the oven to 425°F and put an inverted broiler-pan bottom or baking sheet in to heat.

Roll out the pastry into a rough circle about 10 inches in diameter or into an 8½ by 11-inch rectangle, making either about ³⁄₁₆ inch thick. Place it on a sheet of parchment paper and use your fingers to pinch a high rim all the way around to contain the filling.

Spoon the base filling and your choice of ingredients into the pastry. Open the oven and carefully slide the tart, still on the parchment paper, onto the hot inverted pan. Bake for 25 minutes, until the pastry is golden.

Makes one 10¼-inch tart

1 recipe Semolina Pastry (see page 16)

1 egg, beaten with a pinch of salt, for sealing the pastry

For the filling

7 tablespoons butter   100 g

¾ cup all-purpose flour

4 cups whole or low-fat milk

4 egg yolks

½ cup grated Emmentaler cheese

¼ cup grated Parmesan cheese

2 teaspoons Dijon mustard

sea salt and freshly ground black pepper

½ whole nutmeg, grated (or more, to taste)

1 pound boneless, skinless chicken breasts or thighs   ⌣ 450 g

2 tablespoons light olive oil or canola oil

9 ounces small button mushrooms   255 g

2 tablespoons finely chopped fresh tarragon

1 tablespoon finely chopped fresh parsley

Chicken & tarragon tart

This tart has a really oozy, creamy filling, and makes a great contrast to the semolina pastry, which is a little shorter and crispier than the basic salted pastry, and has a slightly grainy texture.

Rest the pastry in the refrigerator for at least 1 hour, preferably several, or, better still, overnight (see page 29).

Preheat the oven to 375°F.

Lightly grease a 10¼-inch tart pan. Dust your work surface with flour, roll out the pastry ³⁄₁₆ inch thick, and line the pan (see pages 30–36). Line with parchment paper and ceramic baking weights. Put into the refrigerator to rest for 30 minutes. Remove the pan from the refrigerator, place on a baking sheet, and bake for 20 minutes. Lift out the parchment and weights, brush the pastry with the beaten egg, then bake for another 10 minutes (see pages 37–41). Set aside.

Lower the oven to 350°F.

TO MAKE THE FILLING: Melt the butter in a saucepan, add the flour, and cook for 1 minute, whisking all the time. Add the milk gradually, whisking continuously until the mixture comes to a boil. Lower the heat to a simmer and let the mixture

cook, continuing to whisk, for at least 1 minute more, until it thickens. Whisk in the egg yolks, both cheeses, and the mustard, then taste and season with salt, pepper, and nutmeg. Take off the heat and leave to cool.

Cut the chicken into fine strips. Heat the oil in a frying pan and gently cook the chicken for 4–5 minutes; it needs to be cooked through, so cut into a piece to check. Transfer the chicken to drain on paper towels and set aside.

Add the mushrooms to the frying pan and brown them a little (just for a minute or two). Add them to the saucepan, along with the reserved chicken and the herbs, and stir well. Spoon into the pastry crust.

Put the tart back onto the baking sheet and bake for 20–25 minutes, until the filling is golden and just set if you wobble the sheet. You can eat the tart either warm and runny (I love it like this), or put it in the refrigerator to set and eat it cold with a big green salad.

Makes eight 4-inch tarts

1 recipe Spelt Pastry (see page 16)

2 butternut squash

3 tablespoons olive oil

3 eggs, plus 1 egg, beaten with a pinch of salt, for sealing the pastry

1 cup ricotta cheese

3 ounces Parmesan cheese, grated   85 g

1 tablespoon chopped fresh sage

sea salt and freshly ground black pepper

Butternut squash & ricotta tarts

If you like, you can blind bake the pastry crusts 2–3 days in advance and keep them in an airtight container until you are ready to fill and bake them.

Don't throw away the squash seeds, as you can toast them and then use them to decorate the tarts, or you can eat them as a snack, sprinkled with sea salt. Just spread them out on a baking sheet and put them in the oven for the last 8–10 minutes of the roasting time for the squash, until they are lightly toasted.

Rest the pastry in the refrigerator for at least 1 hour, preferably several, or, better still, overnight (see page 29).

Preheat the oven to 400°F.

Cut the squash lengthwise into quarters. Remove the seeds, but don't throw them away (see headnote). Place the squash quarters on a baking sheet and drizzle with the olive oil. Roast in the oven for 40–45 minutes, until the flesh is soft.

Lower the heat to 375°C. Lightly grease eight 4-inch removable-bottomed pans, about ¾ inch deep.

Dust your work surface with flour, roll out the pastry 1/16–⅛ inch thick, and line the pans (see pages 30–36). Line with parchment paper and ceramic baking weights. Place in the refrigerator to rest for at least 30 minutes.

Remove the pans from the refrigerator, place on baking sheets, and bake for 15 minutes. Lift out the parchment and weights, brush the pastry with the beaten egg, then bake for another 8 minutes (see pages 37–41). Set aside.

Lower the heat to 350°F.

Mix the 3 eggs and the ricotta together in a bowl. Stir in the Parmesan and sage.

When the butternut squash is cool enough to handle, scrape the flesh from the skin into a bowl and mash it with a masher or fork. Stir it into the cheese mixture and season with salt and pepper. Spoon the mixture into the pastry crusts, put back onto the baking sheets, and bake in the oven for 20 minutes, until the filling is just set and the pastry is golden brown. Remove and eat warm, or allow to cool and put in the refrigerator to eat cold.

Makes 4 large pasties (about 6¼ inches long), or
10 small pasties (about 4 inches long)

1 recipe Salted Pastry (see page 16), made with
    margarine, not butter

1 medium rutabaga

1 large potato

1 large onion

14 ounces good-quality skirt or chuck steak, diced
    quite small ⌐ 400g

sea salt and freshly ground black pepper

1 egg, beaten with a pinch of salt, for glazing the pastry

Cornish pasties

Originally, the pasty was poor man's food, made for Cornish field workers and miners to take to work with them. As a Breton, I know I am walking into a minefield here because there is so much controversy about what makes an authentic pasty. Although most recipes would have lard in the pastry, I prefer to use my usual salted pastry, though made with margarine (in a block or sticks, not a tub) instead of butter to keep it feeling authentic and give the traditional flaky softness required.

Purists, I know, insist that the filling should be made with turnip, not rutabaga, and that the pasty should be crimped around the side, not over the top. But this is *my* version, and I like crimping over the top because it looks more distinctive and less like an apple turnover.

You can make up the pasties completely, brush them with beaten egg, and then freeze them. Before baking, defrost them completely (allow 3–4 hours, and insert a skewer into the center to check that they are defrosted all the way through), then bake as normal.

Rest the pastry in the refrigerator for at least 1 hour, preferably several, or, better still, overnight (see page 29).

Preheat the oven to 400°F.

Roll out the pastry ¹⁄₁₆–¹⁄₈ inch thick (for small pastries) or ³⁄₁₆ inch thick (for large ones) and cut out circles either 6¼ inches or 4 inches in diameter. (Use a pastry cutter or cut around a plate.) Stack up the circles, interleaving them with waxed paper, and put in the refrigerator while you make the filling.

Peel the rutabaga, potato, and onion, and cut into small cubes around ⅝ inch—don't worry about perfection, but try to keep them roughly the same size so they will cook evenly. Put all the vegetables in a bowl with the diced steak, mix together, and season well with salt, and especially with black pepper.

Divide the filling among the chilled pastry circles, spooning it into the center of each circle. Brush a little water around the edge of the pastry, then bring the sides together and crimp neatly over the top.

Place the pasties on a lightly greased baking sheet and brush them with the beaten egg. With the tip of a sharp knife, make a small hole just to one side of the crimping to allow steam to escape. Bake for 10 minutes, then lower the heat to 350°F and bake for another 30 minutes, until golden brown and the base is brown and firm.

1 recipe Caraway Pastry (see page 16)

For the filling

7 ounces pork belly, skin removed

7 ounces pork shoulder

7 ounces duck leg meat

7 ounces duck liver

6 juniper berries

2 teaspoons whole allspice

1 teaspoon whole green peppercorns

1 teaspoon smoked sweet paprika

¾ teaspoon thyme leaves

Scant 1 cup dry or sweet sherry or port

18 small shallots, unpeeled

light olive oil or canola oil

1 smoked duck breast

2 extra-large eggs

⅔ cup half-and-half

sea salt and freshly ground black pepper

For the jelly

2 tablespoons water

1¾ teaspoons unflavored powdered gelatin

¾ cup plus 2 tablespoons good chicken stock

6½ tablespoons sweet sherry or port

For the topping

3 medium golden (or striped) beets

3 medium red beets

a few sprigs rosemary and thyme

olive oil

Duck pie

This is a fantastic, rich open pie that is finished with a little sherry or port jelly poured into it after baking. It is served cold, topped with roasted beets and shallots, so it looks quite spectacular. You can find beets in all sorts of colors and stripes in good produce stores or farmers' markets, so have fun with the topping. I promise it is much simpler to make than it sounds; you just need to allow plenty of time. Ideally, start the night before: make the pastry and line the pan, then put the meat in a bowl to marinate, and keep both in the refrigerator overnight. If you're pressed for time, a couple of hours in the refrigerator for both is fine, but note that once you have made the pie, cooled it for 2 hours, then poured in the jelly, it will need to go back into the refrigerator to set for another 4–5 hours. For deep game and pork pies like this, I always dust the greased pan with flour, which seems to help the finish of the pastry.

Rest the pastry in the refrigerator for at least 1 hour, preferably several, or, better still, overnight (see page 29).

TO MAKE THE FILLING: Trim and dice the pork belly and shoulder and duck legs and liver and place in a bowl. Add the spices, thyme, and sherry, stir, then leave to marinate for at least 2–3 hours, but preferably overnight, in the refrigerator. Give the bowl a shake from time to time.

Lightly grease an 8-inch removable-bottomed square or round cake pan and pour in a little flour. Tilt the pan around so that every surface is lightly dusted, then tap out the excess.

Remove the pastry from the refrigerator and roll it out on a very lightly floured surface (see pages 30–31) to form a square or circle about ³⁄₁₆ inch thick and twice the size of your pan (i.e., 16 inches square or in diameter).

(Continued)

Lift the pastry over the pan and gently line it (see pages 34–36). Place it back in the refrigerator for at least 30 minutes (or until the meat has finished marinating).

When you are ready to make the pie, preheat the oven to 350°F.

To finish the filling, put the unpeeled shallots in a saucepan with enough oil to cover and simmer very slowly for 10–15 minutes, until they are soft and can be easily pierced with the tip of a knife. Leave to cool, then slice off the base and squeeze from the other end so that the shallots pop out of their skins. Keep the shallot flesh to one side.

Dice the smoked duck breast, then set aside.

Remove the marinated meat from the refrigerator and put through a meat grinder (use the largest holes), or chop finely with a large knife.

Mix the eggs and half-and-half together in a bowl, stir in the minced meat, add the diced duck breast, and season with salt and pepper. To test that it is seasoned to your liking, take a little bit of the mixture and fry it in a pan. Make sure it is cooked through, then taste it and adjust if necessary. Now mix in half of the shallots.

Take your pastry crust out of the refrigerator and fill it with the meat mixture.

Cover the top with a piece of parchment paper to stop the pastry from browning too quickly, place on a baking sheet, and bake for 1½–1¾ hours, until the meat is cooked through. During baking, rotate the pie and move it around the oven if necessary so that the pastry is evenly baked. You can test for doneness by inserting a metal skewer into some pieces of meat and checking that the skewer comes out piping hot. For the last 30 minutes, remove the parchment paper.

Take the pie from the oven and leave to cool for at least 2 hours.

TO MAKE THE JELLY: Pour the water into a small bowl, sprinkle the gelatin over, then let stand for a few minutes.

Heat the stock and sherry in a saucepan over low heat, add the gelatin, and stir well until dissolved. Take off the heat and leave to cool, but not until the jelly becomes too thick to pour.

Now take the cold pie (still in its pan). You will notice that the meat has separated a little from the pastry crust, so pour the sherry jelly into the gap and over the top of the meat. Put the pie in the refrigerator so that the jelly sets. This will take 4–5 hours, but the pie will be at its best after 24 hours (it will keep in the refrigerator for up to 1 week if you don't want to eat it straightaway).

Before serving, heat the oven again to 400°F.

TO MAKE THE TOPPING: Wash the beets and put them whole into a saucepan of water. Bring to a boil, then lower the heat and simmer for about 20 minutes, until you can slide the tip of a knife into the beets, but there is still a bit of resistance. Lift out the beets and, when cool enough to handle, cut into wedges, leaving the peel on and any little bits of root or stalk—these give the wedges character and will make the topping for your pie look even more eye-catching. Place in a baking pan with the rosemary and thyme, drizzle with a little olive oil, and roast in the oven for about 25 minutes, or until tender. Remove and allow to cool.

When the jelly has set, ease the whole pie carefully from the pan, arrange the beet wedges and reserved shallots on top, and serve.

Makes 8

1 egg, beaten with a pinch of salt, for glazing the pastry

For the hot-water crust

1 egg

15.7 ounces all-purpose flour

6.1 ounces lard (or goose or duck fat)

6 ounces water

1 teaspoon salt

1 teaspoon sugar

For the filling

10.5 ounces pork belly, skin removed

10.5 ounces pork shoulder

2 anchovies in oil, drained

2 tablespoons chopped fresh sage

7 ounces bacon or pancetta

½ whole nutmeg, grated

sea salt and freshly ground black pepper

For the jelly

2 tablespoons water

1¾ teaspoons unflavored powdered gelatin

¾ cup plus 2 tablespoons good chicken stock

6½ tablespoons sweet sherry or port

Pork pies

Consider this a bonus recipe that stands apart from the others in this chapter because it uses hot-water crust, which is a different type of pastry from those described previously. It is used only for making raised pies that are eaten cold.

Raised pies are something that the British have always been good at making, from the humble to the elaborate, filled with all kinds of meat, game, and fruit. But the one I loved instantly when I came to England was the individual pure pork pie. Well seasoned and made properly with good-quality meat and great jelly, it is just beautiful.

Traditionally, the jelly is made using a pig's trotter, and there is a recipe for this on page 98. But if you are short of time you can make the simple version here (which I also use for the Duck Pie on page 81). In most traditional recipes, the pastry is also hand-raised, which means that it is shaped without the help of a mold. However, I know that many people find the idea of doing this quite daunting, so these pies are made in a much easier way, in dariole molds (you may substitute 4-ounce ramekins if you cannot find dariole molds).

If you don't want to try the hot-water crust, you could make these pies using Cornish pasty pastry (see page 16). It will obviously have a slightly different flavor and texture, but you will still have some very tasty pies!

(Continued)

TO MAKE THE HOT-WATER CRUST: Break the egg into a small bowl. Put the flour into a large bowl and make a well in the center. Add the egg to the flour and stir in briefly.

Put the lard in a saucepan with the water, salt, and the sugar. Bring to a boil, stirring as the lard melts. When it comes to a boil, count to 30 seconds and immediately take the pan off the heat. Pour the liquid into the flour mixture, stirring continuously with a wooden spoon.

When the mixture forms quite a sticky dough, cover the bowl with a clean dish towel and leave to rest and cool for 1 hour.

Turn the dough onto a lightly floured work surface (see page 23). Flatten it out with your hands.

(Continued)

 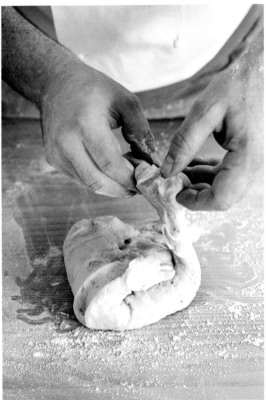

Fold the dough into thirds by taking one side into the center and pressing down with your fingertips.

Next, bring the opposite side over the top.

Press down again with your fingertips.

Flatten the dough into a rough oblong shape, lift onto a baking sheet, then cover with waxed paper and put into the refrigerator to rest for at least 30 minutes.

(Continued)

WHILE THE PASTRY IS RESTING, MAKE THE FILLING: Dice the pork belly and shoulder roughly and mix with the anchovies and sage. Put the mixture through a meat grinder (use the larger holes). Alternatively, place in a food processor and pulse briefly, stopping and starting, until you have a coarse texture. (By pulsing in short bursts, you will avoid overdoing it and ending up with meat paste.) If you don't have a machine, you can chop all the meat very finely with a big knife; it is just a bit more tedious.

Cut the bacon into small pieces and stir it into the ground meat. Add the nutmeg, then season with salt and pepper and mix well. To test that the filling is seasoned to your liking, take a little bit of the mixture and fry it in a pan. Make sure it is cooked through, then taste it and adjust if necessary.

Preheat the oven to 350°F.

Take the pastry out of the refrigerator—by now it should be firmer. Roll it briefly on a lightly floured work surface (see page 30). Fold it into thirds and roll out again about ⅛ inch thick.

Finally, using a pastry cutter or saucer about 5 inches in diameter, cut out eight circles. Now use a cutter or tumbler 3¼ inches in diameter to cut out another eight circles.

(Continued)

Lightly grease eight dariole molds or ramekins, then dust with flour, emptying out the excess. Line each mold with a large circle of pastry, pushing it gently into the base and against the sides, and leaving about ⅜ inch overhanging the rim. An easy way of doing this is to drape your pastry over a smaller inverted mold or glass, then put the dariole mold you want to line over the top.

Turn both over and remove the smaller mold or glass.

With your fingertips, press the pastry well into the base and sides of the mold.

Repeat with the rest of the molds. Now you are ready to fill them.

(Continued)

Divide the meat mixture among the molds, then tap each mold on the work surface to help the meat settle down. Put a small pastry circle over the top of each mold. Starting in the center and working outward to the edges, press it gently onto the meat with your fingertips without stretching it.

Crimp the edges of the pastry together all around, making sure they are firmly sealed.

(Continued)

Brush the top of each pie with the beaten egg, then use a skewer to make a hole in the top of each one to allow steam to escape in the oven.

Place the molds on a baking sheet and bake for 40 minutes, until the meat is cooked through (a skewer inserted into the center of the pies should come out piping hot, or an instant-read thermometer should register 190°F–195°F). Leave the pies to cool for at least 2 hours.

MEANWHILE, MAKE THE JELLY: Add the water to a small bowl, sprinkle the gelatin over, then let stand for a few minutes.

Heat the stock and sherry in a saucepan over low heat, add the gelatin, and stir well until dissolved. Remove from the heat and leave to cool, but not until the jelly becomes too thick to pour.

When the pies are cool, take a little funnel, a piping tip, or a syringe (or make a small cone with some parchment paper) and push it into the hole you made in each pie. Carefully pour in enough jelly to come to the top. Put the pies in the refrigerator for 8 hours to set, then turn out and eat!

Makes about 1 quart

1 pig's trotter or 1 chicken carcass

8 cups water

1 bay leaf

1 carrot

1 onion

6 black peppercorns

1¾ teaspoons unflavored powdered gelatin and 2 tablespoons water, if using a chicken carcass

Traditional pork pie jelly

When you make this with a pig's trotter, it is naturally gelatinous and needs no additional thickening, but if you make it with a chicken carcass, you will need to add some gelatin. This recipe makes a generous amount, and you will need only 1¼ cups of it for the Pork Pie recipe on page 85, so freeze any left over for another occasion.

Place the pig's trotter or chicken carcass, water, bay leaf, carrot, onion, and peppercorns in a saucepan and bring to a boil. Skim the scum from the surface, then lower the heat and simmer for 2 hours, skimming regularly. Remove from the heat and pour the liquid through a sieve into clean saucepan. Bring to a boil and simmer for 10 minutes more to reduce and thicken slightly.

If you have used a chicken carcass rather than a pig's trotter, put the 2 tablespoons water in a small bowl, sprinkle the gelatin over, then let stand for a few minutes. Add a little of the hot liquid to the gelatin and stir to dissolve. Add this to the pan and stir well.

Remove the pan from the heat, leave to cool, then use to fill the pork pies (see page 96).

1 recipe Salted Pastry (see page 16), with whole-grain spelt flour substituted for the all-purpose flour, plus
   1 tablespoon whole-grain spelt

Spelt wafers

These crispy wafers, which are great with cheese, are made with spelt pastry, a variation of salted. I use all whole-grain spelt flour, rather than a mixture of spelt and all-purpose flours, and I add some extra whole-grain spelt so that you get a really good, crunchy texture.

Make the pastry as usual, adding the whole-grain spelt to the spelt flour at the beginning. Rest the pastry, neatly squared off, in the refrigerator for at least 1 hour, preferably several, or, better still, overnight (see page 29). The firmer it is the better.

Preheat the oven to 325°F.

Using a very sharp knife, cut the chilled pastry into wafers 1/16–1/8 inch thick. Lay them on one or more baking sheets and bake for 10–12 minutes. They will be a dark golden color, thanks to the spelt. Remove from the oven and leave to cool and crisp up a little on the sheet(s) before transferring to a rack to cool completely. The wafers will keep in an airtight container for 2–3 weeks.

3   Sweet

My earliest memories of sweet pastries are of Sundays mornings in Brittany when, like most families, we would go to the boulangerie/pâtisserie and choose a selection to have after Sunday lunch; perhaps some apple or apricot tarts, or pear *bourdaloue*, with its frangipane puffed up and golden around the fruit. There might be some choux pastry swans with ruffled chantilly cream "feathers," and in summer always fresh strawberry tarts, with the fruit glistening on a layer of beautiful vanilla crème pâtissière. During the week you might make a simple fruit tart at home, but on Sundays the tradition is still to treat the family to something special, beautifully presented in a box tied with ribbon.

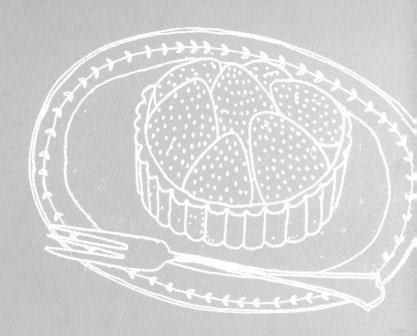

In Britain, there is much more enthusiasm for baking at home any day of the week, and I don't think you can beat a classic sweet tart at any time of the day—with a coffee in the morning, a cup of tea in the afternoon, or as a dessert after dinner. The key is to keep the pastry thin enough in proportion to the topping so that it has an elegant crispness to it.

Most of the tarts that follow can be eaten warm or cold, though by cold I mean at room temperature. So often we have a tendency to eat things when they are piping hot or straight from the refrigerator, and at either extreme, the temperature dulls the flavor. Even if you keep a refreshing fresh fruit tart in the refrigerator, it will taste just a little bit more special if you allow it to come up to room temperature before serving it.

1 recipe Sweet Pastry (see page 17)

1 egg, beaten with a pinch of salt, for sealing the pastry

For the crème pâtissière

1 cup whole milk (low-fat could be used if you prefer, but the cream will not be as rich)

1 vanilla bean

3 egg yolks

5 tablespoons superfine sugar

3 tablespoons all-purpose plain flour

For the fruit filling

dash of kirsch (if using strawberries) or rum (optional)

about 1⅔ pounds strawberries or other fresh fruit

1–2 tablespoons water

about ⅔ cup apricot jam, for glazing

confectioners' sugar, for dusting

fresh mint leaves, for decoration (optional)

Fruit tartlets

These are classic tarts made with fresh fruits on a creamy base. Crème pâtissière—literally "pastry chef's cream"—is often confused with crème anglaise, which is the French name for custard. They are very similar, but whereas custard is set only with eggs, crème pâtissière also uses flour (or cornstarch) so that it is thicker and can be used as a base or filling for all kinds of pastries. It is at the heart of the pastry-maker's craft and you will find it used frequently in the puff pastry chapter as well as here.

I prefer to make my crème pâtissière in the more traditional way, with flour rather than cornstarch. Cornstarch gives more of a sheen, but I feel I can taste it in the finished cream.

The key to making good crème pâtissière is in the final stage. Once the hot milk has been whisked into the eggs, flour, and sugar, it goes back onto the heat, and—this is the important bit—it needs to come to a boil and then kept at a boil for a minute while you whisk continuously. This is what cooks the mixture so that you don't taste any flouriness in the finished cream, and makes it set properly.

I like to teach people how to make these tartlets in my pastry classes, not only because they involve the all-important crème pâtissière, but because once you master making impressive-looking small tartlets, it is easy to move on to bigger ones and feel confident about it.

This recipe makes 24 tartlets. Of course I know most people aren't going to have that many pans, but you can blind bake the crusts in batches 2–3 days in advance if you like, and keep them in an airtight container, ready to fill with the pastry cream and top with fruit when you want to serve them. Or, if you want to make a smaller batch, you can freeze whatever pastry you don't need for another time (see page 63).

The tarts can be made to look very smart by cutting and arranging the various fruits in the way professional pastry chefs do it (see pages 200–204).

(Continued)

Rest the pastry in the refrigerator for at least 1 hour, preferably several, or, better still, overnight (see page 29).

TO MAKE THE CRÈME PÂTISSIÈRE: Put the milk into a heavy-based saucepan. Using a sharp knife, split the vanilla bean along its length, scrape the seeds into the milk, then put the halved pods in too.

Put the egg yolks and sugar into a bowl and whisk until pale and creamy. Add the flour and mix until smooth.

Put the pan of milk over medium heat, bring to just under a boil, then slowly pour half of it into the egg mixture, whisking well as you do so. Add the remainder of the milk and whisk again, then pour the mixture back into the pan. Bring to a boil, whisking all the time, then keep boiling and whisking continuously for 1 minute. Remove from the heat.

Pour the mixture into a clean bowl and scoop out the vanilla pods. (You can wash and dry them and keep them in a jar of sugar, which will give you vanilla-flavored sugar for use in all your baking.) Cover the surface of the bowl with parchment paper straightaway to prevent a skin forming. Allow to cool, then store in the refrigerator until you're ready to use it.

Lightly grease 24 removable-bottomed tart pans, 3¼ inches in diameter and ¾ inch deep. (If you don't have this many pans, you can bake in batches.)

Dust your work surface with flour, roll out the pastry ¹⁄₁₆–⅛ inch thick, and line the pans (see pages 30–36). Line with parchment paper and ceramic baking weights. Place in the refrigerator to rest for at least 30 minutes.

Preheat the oven to 375°F.

Remove the pans from the refrigerator, place on a baking sheet, and bake for 15 minutes. Lift out the parchment and weights, brush the pastry with the beaten egg, then bake for another 8 minutes (see pages 37–41). Set aside. Leave the pastry crusts in the pans for about 15 minutes, then lift out and leave on a rack until cool.

TO MAKE THE FRUIT FILLING: Fill the pastry crusts with crème pâtissière (mixed with a little kirsch, if you like, if using strawberries, or with rum if using another fruit) and top with your fresh fruit.

Put the jam into a saucepan with the water, and bring to just under a simmer. Don't let the mixture boil or the jam will become too gooey to spread properly. Press the jam through a fine sieve to remove any pulp. Using a pastry brush, lightly glaze the top of each tartlet. Alternatively, dust the tartlets with confectioners' sugar.

Decorate, if you like, with mint leaves.

Makes twenty-four 3¼-inch tartlets

1 recipe Sweet Pastry (see page 17)

1 egg, beaten with a pinch of salt, for sealing the pastry

For the filling

7 organic lemons

9 eggs

2 cups superfine sugar

1 cup heavy cream

confectioners' sugar, for glazing (optional)

Lemon tartlets

I like to make small lemon tartlets, but you can make them in other sizes if you wish (see page 17); you might prefer just a big one (10¼ by 1½ inches), which can be cut into slices. You can blind bake the pastry crusts in batches, 2–3 days in advance if you like, and keep them in an airtight container, ready to fill. You can then finish the baking when you want to serve them.

If you have any lemon filling left over, it needn't be wasted: spoon it into ramekins and bake in the same way, but without the pastry. Served with cookies and a little crème fraîche, it makes a lovely pudding.

Rest the pastry in the refrigerator for at least 1 hour, preferably several, or, better still, overnight (see page 29).

Lightly grease 24 removable-bottomed tart pans, 3¼ inches in diameter and ¾ inch deep. (If you don't have this many pans, you can bake in batches.)

Dust your work surface with flour, roll out the pastry 1⁄16–⅛ inch thick, and line the pans (see pages 30–34). Line with parchment paper and ceramic baking weights. Place in the refrigerator to rest for at least 30 minutes.

Preheat the oven to 375°F.

Remove the pans from the refrigerator, place on a baking sheet, and bake for 15 minutes. Lift out the paper and weights, brush the pastry with the beaten egg, then bake for another 8 minutes (see pages 37–41). Set aside.

Lower the oven to 300°F.

TO MAKE THE FILLING: Grate the zest of 4 of the lemons and squeeze the juice from all of them. Whisk the eggs, sugar, and lemon zest in a large bowl until smooth, then add the lemon juice. Lightly whip the cream and fold it into the egg mixture. Skim any froth from the top, then pour into the pastry crusts.

Bake for about 15 minutes, until the filling doesn't wobble if you shake the pans very gently, and the center feels just set when touched. Don't wait until it feels very firm, as it will firm up a little as it cools.

Leave in the pans for about 15 minutes, then lift out and cool on a rack for 2 hours before eating. If you like, before serving, you can dust the top of each tartlet with a little confectioners' sugar and melt with a blowtorch to glaze.

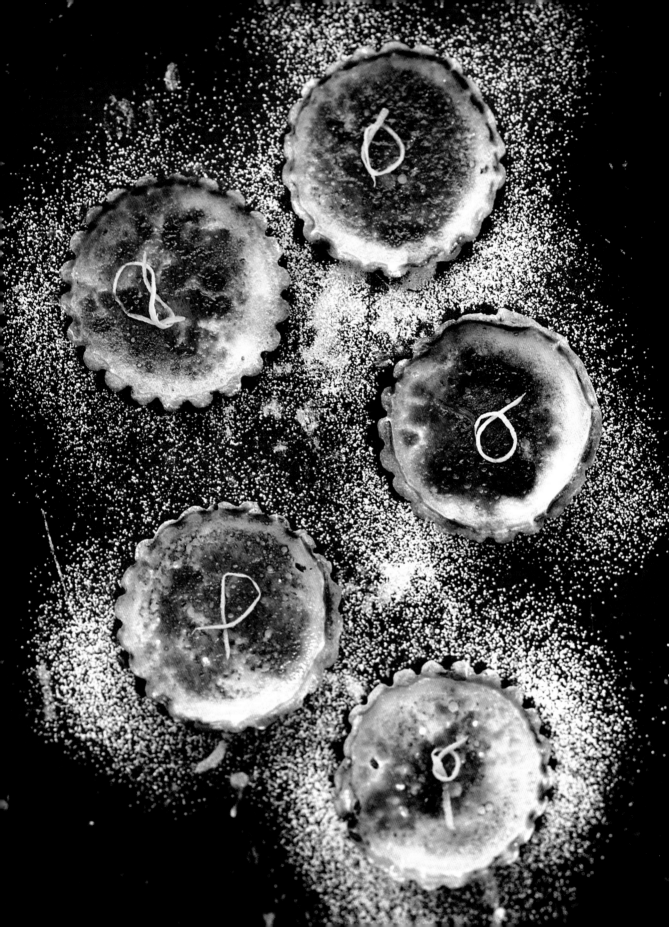

Makes one 14 by 4½-inch tart

1 recipe Chocolate Pastry (see page 17)

12 fresh cherries with stems, 24 cherries preserved in
    alcohol or syrup, or 24 defrosted frozen cherries

6½ tablespoons kirsch, if using canned or frozen cherries

1 egg, beaten with a pinch of salt, for sealing the pastry

For the chocolate filling

¾ cup sugar

4 eggs

4 egg yolks

11¼ ounces good-quality dark chocolate
    (at least 70% cacao)

1½ cups butter   400g

¾ cup all-purpose flour

Unsweetened cocoa powder, for dusting

Chocolate cherry tart

This is a beautiful tart to make when fresh cherries are in season. I like it best when it is still a little warm
and the chocolate is quite soft and gooey, like a good chocolate brownie. But if you like a firmer texture,
you can leave it to cool completely. Either way, it's gorgeous with whipped cream. I think it is fun to leave
the stems on the cherries so that they pop out of the tart.

If you want to make this tart out of season, you can still do it using cherries preserved in alcohol or
syrup. Failing that, you could use frozen or canned cherries, and in both cases soak them in kirsch before
use. However, you will need more preserved cherries than if using fresh because they are less plump and
will disappear more into the chocolate filling.

I like to make the tart rectangular and cut it into squares to serve, but you can make it circular or
any shape you wish.

(Continued)

Rest the pastry in the refrigerator for at least 1 hour, preferably several, or, better still, overnight (see page 29).

If using canned or defrosted cherries, drain them and put them into a bowl with the kirsch. Leave to soak overnight.

Lightly grease a removable-bottomed tart pan, 14 by 4½ inches and ¾ inch deep.

Dust your work surface with flour, roll out the pastry 3/16 inch thick, and line the pan (see pages 30–36). Line with parchment paper and ceramic baking weights. Place in the refrigerator to rest for at least 30 minutes.

MEANWHILE, MAKE THE CHOCOLATE FILLING: In a mixing bowl, whisk the sugar, eggs, and egg yolks until the mixture is pale and has a creamy, mousselike consistency.

Break the chocolate into chunks and put into a heatproof bowl. Place this over a saucepan of simmering water—you need enough water to come close to the bottom of the bowl but not actually touch it. Turn the heat very low so that you don't get steam into the bowl, as this can make the chocolate stiffen and look dull. Let the chocolate melt slowly, stirring all the time, then add the butter and keep stirring until it has melted. Take off the heat and add to the sugar and egg mixture, again stirring well until it is all incorporated. Gently fold in the flour and set aside.

Preheat the oven to 375°F.

Remove the pan from the refrigerator, place on a baking sheet and bake for 20 minutes. Lift out the parchment and baking weights, brush the pastry with the beaten egg, then bake for another 10 minutes (see pages 37–41). Set aside to cool.

Lower the oven to 350°F.

Spread the filling over the cooled pastry up to the top, then push the cherries into it, leaving some of the fruit showing (if using fresh cherries, leave the stems sticking out). Put back on the baking sheet and return to the oven for 12 minutes, until just set. The filling will have risen a little, but, like a chocolate brownie, it should be only just firm to the touch, as it will set a bit more when it cools. Leave in the pan for about 15 minutes, then lift out and cool on a rack.

The tart can be served either warm and gooey, or completely cooled, when the chocolate will be a bit firmer. Dust with cocoa powder before serving.

Variation

Use sliced ripe (or canned) pears instead of cherries.

Makes twenty-four 3¼-inch tartlets

1 recipe Sweet or Lemon Pastry (see page 17)

1 egg, beaten with a pinch of salt, for sealing the pastry

For the lemon curd filling

juice and grated zest of 3 organic lemons

3 extra-large eggs

1 cup superfine sugar

½ cup butter   113 g

1 teaspoon cornstarch

For the meringue

6 egg whites

1¾ cups granulated sugar

5 tablespoons water

Lemon meringue tartlets

These tartlets are filled with lemon curd, but you could use the lemon filling from the recipe on page 108, if you like. Of course you can make a bigger tart (see page 17), but I think small tartlets are more fun because you can be a bit wild with the meringue. You can blind bake the pastry crusts in batches, 2–3 days in advance, and keep them in an airtight container, ready to fill. You can then finish the baking when you want to serve them.

Rest the pastry in the refrigerator for at least 1 hour, preferably several, or, better still, overnight (see page 29).

TO MAKE THE LEMON CURD: Whisk all of the ingredients together in a bowl, then place over a saucepan of simmering water. Make sure the water doesn't actually touch the base of the bowl. Heat very gently, whisking all the time and making sure you move the mixture around so it doesn't stick to the sides. Be patient, otherwise you will end up with scrambled eggs (if this should happen, put the mixture through a fine sieve very quickly, then back onto the heat). When the mixture starts to look a little thicker than heavy cream, cook for 1 minute more and it should be ready. To test, blob a little of the mixture onto the inside of the bowl toward the top. It should stay still without dripping. Set aside to cool.

Lightly grease 24 removable-bottomed tart pans, 3¼ inches in diameter and ¾ inch deep. (If you don't have this many pans, you can bake in batches.)

Dust your work surface with flour, roll out the pastry ¹⁄₁₆–⅛ inch thick, and use to line the pans (see pages 30–34). Line with parchment paper and ceramic baking weights. Place in the refrigerator to rest for at least 30 minutes.

Preheat the oven to 375°F.

Remove the pans from the refrigerator, place on baking sheets, and bake for 15 minutes. Lift out the parchment and baking weights, brush the pastry with the beaten egg, then bake for another 8 minutes (see pages 37–41). Set aside to cool.

(Continued)

Fill each pastry crust halfway with lemon curd and put into the refrigerator until set.

MEANWHILE, MAKE THE MERINGUE: Whisk the egg whites until they form soft peaks. Put the sugar into a saucepan with the water and bring to a boil over medium heat. At first you will see large bubbles; after 5–8 minutes, when some of the water has evaporated, the bubbles will be smaller. At this point you will have a thin, colorless syrup (if you have a candy thermometer, the syrup should register 250°F).

Wrap a dish towel around the bowl of egg whites and wedge it into a second saucepan or larger bowl on your work surface so that it is held steady. Using one hand, pour in the hot sugar syrup in a steady stream while whisking with the other hand, until the mixture becomes shiny and forms proper peaks. (Alternatively, you can whisk the egg whites in a stand mixer fitted with the whisk attachment, and add the sugar syrup with the motor running.)

Fit a piping bag with a star tip (see page 61) and fill with meringue. Take the pastry crusts from the refrigerator and pipe meringue over the lemon curd, going around and upward to create peaks that are as wild as you like.

As the egg in the meringue has already been cooked by the hot syrup, the tarts need no further baking, but I think the meringue looks smarter and has more definition if the tips are lightly browned. The best way to do this is with a blowtorch, as it allows you to control which areas of the meringue you color. The browning could also be done under a broiler or in a hot oven (400°F), but watch carefully to make sure the meringue doesn't burn.

Makes eight 4-inch cheesecakes

1 recipe Sweet Pastry (see page 17)

1 egg, beaten with a pinch of salt, for sealing the pastry

For the filling

1 pound cream cheese   450 g

1 cup superfine sugar

seeds from 1 large vanilla bean or 1 teaspoon vanilla extract

4 eggs

2 egg yolks

14 ounces (1¾ cups) mascarpone cheese   400g

2 teaspoons all-purpose flour

Mascarpone cheesecakes

I wasn't a huge fan of cheesecake until I tasted the one made by Ronnie Bonetti at Babington House in Somerset. Inspired by his original recipe, I came up with the variations below. Of course you can make one big cheesecake if you prefer (see photo on page 62).

Rest the pastry in the refrigerator for at least 1 hour, preferably several, or, better still, overnight (see page 29).

Lightly grease eight 4 by ¾-inch removable-bottomed tart pans.

Dust your work surface with flour, roll out the pastry ¹⁄₁₆–⅛ inch thick, and line the pans (see pages 30–36). Line with parchment paper and ceramic baking weights. Place in the refrigerator to rest for at least 30 minutes.

Preheat the oven to 375°F.

Remove the pans from the refrigerator, place on baking sheets, and bake for 15 minutes. Lift out the parchment and ceramic weights, brush the pastry with the beaten egg, then bake for another 8 minutes (see pages 37–41). Set aside. Lower the oven to 300°F.

TO MAKE THE FILLING: Put the cream cheese, sugar, and vanilla into a bowl and beat until smooth. Beat in the eggs and yolks, then add the mascarpone,

stirring until just incorporated. Fold in the flour. Divide the filling among the tart crusts, put back on the baking sheets, and bake for 45 minutes, until just set. Leave in the pans for about 15 minutes, then lift out and cool on a rack.

Variations

Passion fruit cheesecakes: Take 4 or 5 ripe passion fruits, cut them in half, and scrape the pulp into a small saucepan. Warm gently without boiling. Stir into the mascarpone mixture after you have folded in the flour.

Lemon cheesecakes: Omit the vanilla bean and mix the juice and grated zest of 2 organic lemons with the eggs and egg yolks before adding them to the cream cheese mixture.

Black currant (or other red fruit) cheesecakes: Put 9 ounces ripe fruit in a small saucepan, crush slightly with a fork, and warm gently, just to release the juices. Fill the pastry crusts with the mascarpone mixture, then pour the fruit and juices over each one, swirling the top with a small knife.

9 oz → 255 g

Makes four 6¼-inch tarts

1 recipe Sweet or Almond Pastry (see page 17)

3 tablespoons sliced almonds

confectioners' sugar, for dusting, or apricot glaze (see
pages 105–106)

For the almond cream

1 cup plus 1½ tablespoons butter   *240 g*

1¼ cups superfine sugar

2½ cups ground almonds

6 tablespoons all-purpose flour

3 eggs

2 tablespoons Poire Williams liqueur or rum

confectioners' sugar, for dusting

Amandine

This is the classic almond tart made with *crème d'amande* (almond cream, also known as frangipane) and topped with sliced almonds. It is very like Bakewell tart, in which the pastry is filled with frangipane and jam, but without the layer of jam, and the name sounds more chic! A slice with coffee is just brilliant. The almond cream also forms the basis of many of the fruit tarts that follow. I even use it is a topping for my mince pies (see page 136). While you can mix the cream by hand, it is easier to get it light and fluffy with a stand mixer.

One of the great things about making tarts with almond cream is that they freeze well, so virtually any in which it is used can be fully baked and then frozen. When needed, simply defrost (allow 1–2 hours), then put into a preheated oven at 350°F for about 6 minutes to freshen them up and recrisp the pastry a little.

Alternatively, you can make up the tarts completely, ready to bake, and *then* freeze them. Just place them on a baking sheet, loosely cover with an opened-out resealable plastic bag, and freeze until hard, then stack them between layers of parchment paper in an airtight container. They can then be baked without defrosting. The pastry may not be quite as crispy, having been baked from frozen, but it will still be very good. The best way to bake the tarts from frozen is to turn on your oven to 350°F, as the recipe directs, but instead of waiting for it to heat up, put the tarts in straightaway. As the oven comes up to temperature, it will be defrosting the tarts, and they will bake through evenly without coloring too quickly. They will probably take a little longer—around 30 minutes—though this can vary, depending on how quickly your oven heats up, so keep an eye on them. You can check that they are baked all the way through by inserting a skewer into the middle and checking that it is hot. Turn up the heat to 400°F for the last 5 minutes or so, just to get the almond cream nicely colored.

(Continued)

Rest the pastry in the refrigerator for at least 1 hour, preferably several, or, better still, overnight (see page 29).

TO MAKE THE ALMOND CREAM: Beat the butter until very soft, preferably in a stand mixer. With the motor running, add the sugar and ground almonds and mix some more. Now mix in the flour, then the eggs, and finally the liqueur. Transfer to a small bowl and put in the refrigerator for 15 minutes.

Meanwhile, preheat the oven to 350°F.

Lightly grease four 6¼-inch tart rings or removable-bottomed pans (¾ inch deep).

Dust your work surface with flour, roll out the pastry ³⁄₁₆ inch thick, and line the rings (set on baking sheets) or pans (see pages 30–36). Place in the refrigerator to rest for at least 30 minutes then remove and fill with the almond cream. I like to do this with a piping bag, but you can spoon it in and smooth the surface if you prefer.

Top with the sliced almonds, place on baking sheets (if using tart pans), and bake for 20 minutes, until golden brown. Leave in the pans for about 15 minutes.

Trim off the overhanging pastry, then lift out and cool on a rack. Dust with confectioners' sugar before serving.

Makes four 6¼-inch tarts

1 recipe Sweet or Almond Pastry (see page 17)

2½ cups sugar

2 rosemary sprigs, plus more for decoration

4 cups plus 1–2 tablespoons water

10 peaches

1 recipe Almond Cream (see page 119)

about ⅔ cup apricot jam, for glazing (optional)

Peach & rosemary almond tarts

Peach and rosemary might sound like an unusual combination, but the flavors of the fruit and herb work really well together—though you could substitute some sprigs of thyme or lavender if you prefer.

Granulated sugar is much cheaper than superfine sugar, and is fine for making things such as syrups. The syrup used to poach the peaches in this recipe can be stored in the refrigerator and simply boiled again when you want to use it for another recipe. Remember to skim off any impurities that come to the surface, and add a little water if the syrup needs to be thinner. It can also be used instead of apricot jam to glaze the tarts (see the variation).

If you wish, you can fill the pastry crusts with almond cream, then freeze them, ready to bake. Alternatively, you can bake them, then freeze, defrost, and warm them through (see page 119) before poaching the peaches.

(Continued)

Rest the pastry in the refrigerator for at least 1 hour, preferably several, or, better still, overnight (see page 29).

Put the sugar and 2 rosemary sprigs in a saucepan with 4 cups of the water and bring to a boil. Lower the heat and simmer until you have a colorless syrup.

Put the whole peaches into the syrup, bring to just below a simmer, then cook very gently for 20 minutes. Take off the heat and leave to cool.

Lightly grease four 6¼-inch removable-bottomed tart pans (¾ inch deep).

Dust your work surface with flour, roll out the pastry ³⁄₁₆ inch thick, and line the pans (see pages 30–34). Place in the refrigerator to rest for at least 30 minutes.

Preheat the oven to 350°F.

Using a spoon or piping bag, fill the pastry crusts with the almond cream, then place on baking sheets and bake for about 30 minutes, until golden. Leave in the pans for about 15 minutes, then lift out and cool on a rack.

Remove the peaches from the syrup (reserve the syrup), peel the fruits, then cut in half carefully, as they can be a bit fragile. Remove and discard the pits.

With a skewer, make small holes in the baked almond cream and gently pour about 1–2 tablespoons of the syrup over each tart so it soaks in.

If making the apricot glaze, put the jam into a saucepan with the 1–2 tablespoons water and bring to just under a simmer. Don't let the mixture boil or the jam will become too gooey to spread properly. Press the jam through a fine sieve to remove any pulp. (Alternatively, make the syrup glaze below.) Using a pastry brush, lightly glaze the top of each tart; this will give the fruit something to stick to. Place 5 peach halves cut side down, on top of each tart, then glaze a bit more. Push small sprigs of rosemary into the fruit to decorate.

Variation

POACHING SYRUP GLAZE: Add 1½ tablespoons water to a small bowl, sprinkle with 1⅛ teaspoons unflavored powdered gelatin, then let stand for a few minutes. Put 1 cup of the syrup into a small saucepan, simmer to reduce it a bit, then remove from the heat. Add a little of the hot syrup to the gelatin mixture and stir until the gelatin has dissolved, then mix into the rest of the syrup. Leave to cool, then brush over the tarts.

Makes twenty-four 3¼-inch tartlets

1 recipe Sweet Pastry (see page 17)

2½ cups sugar

4 cups plus 2 tablespoons water

12 small ripe pears or 6 large ones, preferably Barlett
  or Comice

1 recipe Almond Cream (see page 119)

⅔ cup apricot jam, for glazing (optional)

Pear Bourdaloue

There are many stories about how this got its name. The most likely is that it is named after La Pâtisserie Bourdaloue on rue Bourdaloue in Paris, where the recipe is said to have first been made in the early 1900s.

People often ask me how to make these classic pear tarts, filled with beautifully soft fruit, as you see them in virtually every French boulangerie/pâtisserie. The secret of the soft fruit is that they are usually made with canned pears. That's not so surprising when you remember that fresh pears are only in season during the autumn. The canned ones are fine, but when the fresh ones are around, I like to poach them in syrup, as in this recipe. The syrup can then be stored in the refrigerator and reused for both poaching and glazing (see page 124).

The recipe is for 24 small tartlets, but if you don't have that many pans, you can bake them in batches and freeze them until needed. Then you can defrost them and warm them through, ready for glazing.

Rest the pastry in the refrigerator for at least 1 hour, preferably several, or, better still, overnight (see page 29).

Bring the sugar and 4 cups of the water to a boil in a saucepan, then simmer until you have a colorless syrup.

Peel the pears, keeping them whole, and put them into the syrup. Simmer gently for 20 minutes, then remove from the heat and leave to cool.

Lightly grease 24 removable-bottomed tart pans, 3¼ inches in diameter and ¾ inch deep.

Dust your work surface with flour, roll out the pastry ¹⁄₁₆–⅛ inch thick, and line the pans (see pages 30–36). Place in the refrigerator to rest for at least 30 minutes.

Preheat the oven to 350°F. Halve the pears if small, or cut them into quarters if large. Place them, rounded side up, on the chopping board, then make several widthwise cuts that go about two-thirds of the way through the flesh. Press down gently and the pear will fan out a little.

Remove the pans from the refrigerator and, using a spoon or piping bag, fill each pastry crust halfway with almond cream. Arrange a fanned pear on top.

Place on baking sheets and bake for about 25 minutes, until the almond cream is golden. Leave in the pans for about 15 minutes, then lift out and cool on a rack.

If making the apricot glaze, put the jam into a saucepan with the remaining 2 tablespoons water and bring to just under a simmer. Don't let the mixture boil or the jam will become too gooey to spread properly. Press the jam through a fine sieve to remove any pulp. Using a pastry brush, lightly glaze the top of each tart.

Makes four 6¼-inch tarts

1 recipe Sweet Pastry (see page 17)

1¼ cups sugar

2 cups plus 1–2 tablespoons water

6 rhubarb stalks, cut into 2½–3-inch lengths

1 recipe Almond Cream (see page 119)

1 tablespoon crème de cassis

1 pint white or red currants

about ⅔ cup apricot jam, for glazing (optional)

Rhubarb & currant tarts

This is a very simple but chic combination: the pink of the rhubarb and pearly white "necklace" of currants give it quite a feminine appeal. Lightly poached rhubarb is a favorite of mine, and the recipe came about when I had some of the early season, bright pink, forced rhubarb (a speciality of West Yorkshire) in the kitchen, and decided to use it as a topping for an almond tart. I felt that an extra flavor and color was needed, so I added some white currants that I also happened to have on hand. It has become one of my favorite tarts. If you wish, you can fill the pastry crusts with almond cream, then freeze them, ready to bake. Alternatively, you can bake and then freeze them until needed. Just defrost and warm them through (see page 119) before poaching the rhubarb. You can use the poaching syrup for a glaze (see page 124).

Rest the pastry in the refrigerator for at least 1 hour, preferably several, or, better still, overnight (see page 29).

Put the sugar and 2 cups of the water into a saucepan and bring to a boil, stirring to dissolve the sugar. Lower the heat and simmer for about 20 minutes, until you have a colorless syrup.

Add the rhubarb and cook for 4–5 minutes, until it has softened but still offers resistance when you pierce it with a sharp knife.

Using a slotted spoon, transfer the rhubarb to a rack placed over a baking sheet to drain and cool. Set aside the pan of poaching syrup.

Preheat the oven to 350°F.

Lightly grease four 6¼-inch removable-bottomed tart pans (¾ inch deep), preferably fluted.

Dust your work surface with flour, roll out the pastry ³⁄₁₆ inch thick, and line the pans (see pages 30–36). Place in the refrigerator to rest for at least 30 minutes.

Using a spoon or piping bag, fill the pastry crusts with the almond cream, then place on baking sheets and bake for about 30 minutes, until golden. Leave in the pans for about 15 minutes, then lift out and cool on a rack.

Mix the crème de cassis with 1 tablespoon of the poaching syrup. Prick the top of each tart with a skewer, then pour the liquid over the almond cream, dividing it evenly and letting it soak in. Arrange the rhubarb and currants on top.

If making the apricot glaze, put the jam into a saucepan with the remaining 1–2 tablespoons water and bring to just under a simmer. Don't let the mixture boil or the jam will become too gooey to spread properly. Press the jam through a fine sieve to remove any pulp. Using a pastry brush, lightly glaze the top of each tart.

Makes eight 4-inch tarts

1 recipe Sweet Pastry (see page 17)

3 tablespoons rum

8 cups hard cider

3 tablespoons Calvados

6 heaping tablespoons brown sugar

6 apples, unpeeled and quartered

1 recipe Almond Cream (see page 119), made with Calvados rather than Poire Williams or rum

Tarte Normande

This is really two recipes in one. Every year at home we make a hot punch for Christmas, which is also brilliant for poaching apples for tarte Normande—and then for drinking with a slice of it.

If you wish, you can make the tarts up completely, then freeze them until you are ready to bake. Alternatively, you can bake and then freeze them until needed. Just defrost and warm them through (see page 119) before serving.

I like to eat tarte Normande at room temperature with crème fraîche, but sometimes I also pour a little warmed Calvados over the tart just before serving, which makes it extra special.

Rest the pastry in the refrigerator for at least 1 hour, preferably several, or, better still, overnight (see page 29).

Pour the rum, cider, and Calvados into a saucepan, add the brown sugar, and warm over low heat, just as if you were making a hot punch or mulled wine—the alcohol shouldn't even bubble. Put in the apples and let them sit in the punch over the lowest heat for several hours so that they soften and soak up the flavors.

Lightly grease eight 4-inch removable-bottomed tart pans (¾ inch deep).

Dust your work surface with flour, roll out the pastry ¹⁄₁₆–⅛ inch thick, and line the pans (see pages 30–36). Place in the refrigerator to rest for at least 30 minutes.

Preheat the oven to 350°F.

Using a spoon or piping bag, fill the pastry crusts with the almond cream. Lift the apples from the punch, and core and slice thinly. Arrange the apple slices in a circular fashion on the almond cream, dividing them evenly.

Place on baking sheets and bake for 20–25 minutes, until the almond cream is golden brown. Leave in the pans for about 15 minutes, then lift out and cool on a rack to room temperature before eating.

Makes eight 4-inch tarts

1 recipe Sweet Pastry (see page 17)

about 24 prunes in rum (see headnote)

1 recipe Almond Cream (see page 119)

3 tablespoons sliced almonds

Prune & rum tarts

In my kitchen, I always have big jars of prunes soaked in rum. They make great treats to serve with coffee during the morning break in pastry classes—and everyone who stops by the kitchen falls in love with them, too. If I can escape for a day's fishing or shooting on the weekend, the gamekeeper always appreciates a jar of them, and a spoonful added to porridge in the morning is a fantastic wake-up call.

All you do is empty a big bag of ready-to-eat prunes into a clean jar, add enough good dark rum to cover, then leave for at least a week, topping up with more prunes as you eat them, or more rum as you drink it.

When making vanilla ice cream, I sometimes pop in a few of the prunes toward the end of churning, and the softest ones, squashed into sweet pastry crusts, topped with almond cream and then baked, make beautiful tarts.

If you wish, you can make the tarts up completely, then freeze them until you are ready to bake. Alternatively, you can bake and then freeze them until needed. Just defrost and warm them through (see page 119) before serving.

Rest the pastry in the refrigerator for at least 1 hour, preferably several, or, better still, overnight (see page 29).

Lightly grease eight 4-inch removable-bottomed tart pans (¾ inch deep).

Dust your work surface with flour, roll out the pastry ¹⁄₁₆–⅛ inch thick, and line the pans (see pages 30–36). Place in the refrigerator to rest for at least 30 minutes.

Preheat the oven to 350°F.

Squash some of the prunes into each pastry crust, then cover with almond cream and sprinkle with sliced almonds. Place on baking sheets and bake for 25–30 minutes, until the almond cream is golden. Serve warm.

Makes 36 tartlets or 1 large tart

1 recipe Pistachio Pastry (see page 17)

½ recipe Almond Cream (see page 119)

½ recipe Crème Pâtissière (see page 105)

about ⅔ cup apricot jam, for glazing

1 tablespoon water

2 pints raspberries

½ cup ground pistachios

Raspberry & pistachio tartlets

While these tartlets are simple to make, the bright green from the pistachios and the red of the raspberries make them look quite spectacular and summery—one big tart also looks pretty dramatic, if you prefer.

If you wish, you can fill the pastry crusts with almond cream, then freeze them, ready to bake. Alternatively, you can bake and then freeze them until needed. Just defrost and warm them through (see page 119). Let them cool before adding the raspberries and pistachios.

Rest the pastry in the refrigerator for at least 1 hour, preferably several, or, better still, overnight (see page 29).

Lightly grease three 12-hole tartlet pans (if you don't have enough pans, bake in batches) or a 7¾-inch square pan, about 1 inch deep.

Flour your work surface and roll out the pastry ¹⁄₁₆–⅛ inch thick for tartlets or ³⁄₁₆ inch thick for a large tart. Use it to line your pan(s) (see pages 33–36), then put into the refrigerator to rest for 30 minutes.

Preheat the oven to 350°F.

Mix the almond cream and crème pâtissière together in a bowl. Using a spoon or piping bag, fill the pastry crusts to the top with the mixture. Bake the tartlets for 15–20 minutes and the large tart for 25–30 minutes, until golden brown.

Leave to cool in the pans for 15 minutes before lifting out and cooling on a rack.

Put the jam into a saucepan with the water and bring to just under a simmer. Don't let the mixture boil or the jam will become too gooey to spread properly. Press the jam through a fine sieve to remove any pulp. Using a pastry brush, lightly glaze the top of the tartlets or tart.

To decorate tartlets, sprinkle the tops with the ground pistachios, then glaze lightly. Place a row of raspberries down the middle and lightly glaze again.

To decorate a large square tart, arrange lines of raspberries in the center and sprinkle a border of ground pistachios all around them (see photo on page 201). Lightly glaze again.

Makes 36

1 recipe Sweet Pastry (see page 17)

14-ounce jar deluxe mincemeat

1 recipe Almond Cream (see page 119)

sliced almonds, for decoration (optional)

confectioners' sugar, for dusting

Frangipane mince pies

I had never seen anything like mince pies when I was growing up in France, but I absolutely love them. My only complaint is that they are often made with too much pastry in relation to the filling, so one Christmas I experimented with covering the pies instead with frangipane (almond cream) flavored with rum and topped with sliced almonds. They went so well that we now make batches of them to sell in our bakery in Bath, and also in the Saturday shop at the cookery school, and I can barely keep up with the demand.

The baked pies can be made 2–3 months in advance and frozen between layers of waxed paper in an airtight container until Christmas. They can then be defrosted and warmed at 325°F for 6–7 minutes to heat through, or eaten at room temperature.

Rest the pastry in the refrigerator for at least 1 hour, preferably several, or, better still, overnight (see page 29).

Lightly grease three 12-hole tartlet pans (if you don't have enough pans, bake in batches).

Flour your work surface and roll out the pastry ¹⁄₁₆–¹⁄₈ inch thick. Using a round cutter or tumbler just larger than the holes in the pan, cut out circles of pastry and line your pans (see pages 30–36). Put into the refrigerator to rest for 30 minutes.

Preheat the oven to 350°F.

Fill the pastry crusts halfway with mincemeat, then pipe about 1 heaping teaspoon almond cream over each one. (Alternatively, spoon it on and smooth over the top.) Sprinkle with a few sliced almonds, if you like.

Bake for about 25 minutes, until golden brown. Leave in the pans for about 15 minutes, then lift out and cool on a rack. Dust with confectioners' sugar.

A Boxful of Sweet Cookies

Sweet pastry can easily be adapted to make a range of cookies. The following recipes are quick to put together, and the resulting cookies will keep for 2–3 weeks in an airtight container—though I never understand how anyone manages to make them last that long. In my family, the moment they are made they are gone! When you bake cookies, instead of using greased baking sheets, you might want to try silicone mats, which are perfect for the job.

Makes 24–36, depending on size

1 recipe Sweet Pastry, or any variation of your choice (see page 17)

1 egg, beaten with a pinch of salt, for glazing

Everyday cookies

There is no rule about which pastry dough to use for these cookies—they can be made in all kinds of flavors and shapes. If you are using the basic sweet pastry dough, you could mix some chocolate chips or pieces of candied citrus peel into it just before resting it. If you are using one of its variations, such as the chocolate pastry dough, you could add some sliced almonds or pieces of walnut. It really is up to you. Similarly, you can use whatever shaped cutters you like, so they are fun to make with children.

Rest the pastry dough in the refrigerator for at least 1 hour, preferably several, or, better still, overnight (see page 29).

Preheat the oven to 350°F and grease two baking sheets.

Lightly flour your work surface and roll out the pastry 1/16 inch thick if you want thin cookies, or about 1/8 inch if you prefer them a little thicker. Cut into squares of about 2½ inches, or use a similar-size cutter to stamp out whatever shape you like. Dust off any excess flour with a pastry brush, then place on the prepared baking sheets and brush with the beaten egg. Bake for 12–15 minutes, depending on the shape and thickness, until golden.

Makes about 24

1 recipe Sweet Pastry (see page 17), but add the grated zest of 2 oranges with the flour or the
     zest of 1 orange and a few drops of orange flower water after adding the butter

1 egg, beaten with a pinch of salt, for glazing

1 recipe Chocolate Crème Pâtissière (see page 208)

Orange & chocolate cookies

These are little sandwiches of orange-flavored cookies filled with chocolate crème patissière. You can make the cookies and keep them for 2–3 weeks in an airtight container before sandwiching them with the filling, but once you add the crème pâtissière, you need to eat them on the same day.

The cookies are flavored either with orange zest or a combination of zest and orange flower water.

Rest the pastry in the refrigerator for at least 1 hour, preferably several, or, better still, overnight (see page 29).

Preheat the oven to 350°F. Lightly grease one or two baking sheets.

Lightly flour your work surface and roll out the pastry ¹⁄₁₆ inch thick if you want thin cookies, or about ⅛ inch if you prefer them a little thicker. Cut into an even number of squares of about 2½ inches, or use a similar-size cutter to stamp out whatever shape you like. Dust off any excess flour, then place on the prepared baking sheets and brush with the beaten egg. Bake for 12–15 minutes, depending on the shape and thickness, until golden. Sandwich the chocolate crème pâtissière between the squares.

Makes about 24

1 recipe Sweet Pastry (see page 17), but use 3 egg yolks instead of 2 eggs and 1 yolk, add 4 teaspoons baking powder to the flour, omit the salt, and use 8.8 ounces salted butter instead of 4.4 ounces unsalted butter

1 egg, beaten with a pinch of salt, for glazing

250 *125g*

Breton biscuits

I grew up in Brittany with cookies like these, made with local salted butter. They are gorgeous, made using the basic sweet pastry method but with double the quantity of butter. You need a good butter flavored with sea salt. I use Breton butter, made with sea salt flakes, which is just beautiful and sold in most good shops and supermarkets. I also put a little baking powder in with the flour for this recipe, so the cookies rise very slightly, and use only egg yolks rather than whole eggs. (You can use the leftover egg whites in the Italian Cookies on page 145.)

Rest the pastry dough in the refrigerator for at least 1 hour, preferably several, or, better still, overnight (see page 29). As you are using double the quantity of butter, the dough needs a long time to set.

Lightly grease two baking sheets. Flour your work surface and roll out the dough about ⅛ inch thick. Use a 2½–3-inch round cutter or tumbler to stamp out circles. Brush off any excess flour, then place on the prepared baking sheets and brush with the beaten egg. Using a fork, make wavy patterns on the top of each cookie, then put into the refrigerator for 30 minutes to firm up again before baking.

Preheat the oven to 350°F. Bake the cookies for 12–15 minutes, until golden.

1 recipe Sweet Pastry (see page 17), but use only 1 egg yolk rather than 2 eggs and 1 yolk,

and add 2.1 ounces semolina to the flour

60

Shortbread

Everyone loves shortbread, and it is so easy to make—just one step beyond the rubbing-in stage for sweet pastry. Then all you have to do is press the crumbly mixture into a baking pan and put it into the oven. That's it! I usually cut the slab of shortbread into classic finger shapes, which means none of it is wasted, but you could use a cutter to stamp out shapes of your choice if you prefer.

When making the sweet pastry dough, work the butter into the flour until the mixture resembles fine bread crumbs.

Add the sugar and the egg yolk. The mixture will be crumbly and a little sticky, like the topping for a fruit crumble.

Preheat the oven to 300°F and line a deep 9½-by-7-inch baking pan with parchment paper.

Transfer the dough to the prepared baking pan and press down gently, easing the mixture into the edges and corners so that you have a flat layer about ⅝ inch deep. Prick all over with a fork, then bake for 45–50 minutes. When it is ready, the shortbread should be very lightly colored.

Remove the pan from the oven and leave to cool a little. Carefully lift out the shortbread, still on the parchment paper, and use a sharp knife to cut it widthwise into 12 strips about ¾ inch wide. Cut in half across the middle so that you end up with 24 fingers.

Makes 36–40

10.5 ounces confectioners' sugar, plus a little extra for rolling out   *300 g*

10.5 ounces ground almonds   *300 g*

2 teaspoons honey

3 egg whites

leftover apricot jam, Crème Pâtissière (see page 105), or sliced almonds, for finishing

Italian cookies

Think of this as another bonus recipe. It is a variation on amaretti, and although it doesn't follow the usual sweet pastry method, it is perfect for using up any egg whites, crème pâtissière, or apricot glaze left over from other recipes.

Mix the confectioners' sugar and ground almonds together. Add the honey and egg whites and mix until you have a smooth, firm dough. Leave to rest in the refrigerator for at least 30 minutes.

Preheat the oven to 300°F and lightly grease two baking sheets.

Divide the dough into four equal pieces. Dust your work surface with confectioners' sugar and roll each piece of dough into a rough sausage shape, about 1 inch in diameter and 8 inches long. Slice each sausage into 8–10 equal pieces.

Lay the rounds of dough on the prepared baking sheets, then gently press your thumb into the center of each so that it leaves an indent. Fill the indents with a little jam, crème pâtissière, or sliced almonds. Bake for about 15 minutes.

To test if the cookies are ready, take the baking sheets out of the oven and tap them lightly on a work surface. The cookies should release themselves from the baking sheets. Leave to cool.

Makes about 24

3.9 ounces butter, softened and cut into pieces	110 g
grated zest of 1 lemon or orange	
3.9 ounces superfine sugar	110 g
3 egg whites	
3.9 ounces all-purpose flour	110 g
1 drop vanilla extract	

Langues de chat

Like the previous recipe, this one also makes good use of egg whites left over from making pastry. These classic fine, crisp cookies take their name from their shape, which is supposed to resemble a cat's tongue, and they are really simple to make.

Take the butter out of the refrigerator in advance to soften it, or use the rolling pin method (see page 18), rather than put it in the microwave and risk it becoming oily.

In a bowl, beat the butter with the lemon zest until soft. Add the sugar and continue to beat until pale and creamy, scraping the mixture from the sides of the bowl as you do so. Gradually beat in the egg whites and, finally, the flour, until you have a smooth paste. Stir in the vanilla and rest the mixture in the refrigerator for at least 2 hours.

Preheat the oven to 300°F and grease two baking sheets.

You can either pipe the mixture, which gives neatly shaped cookies, or you can spoon it, which will give more interesting, slightly uneven shapes. It is up to you. If you decide to pipe the mixture, fill a piping bag fitted with a very small plain tip (see page 61) and pipe strips of 2½–2¾ inches (or longer if you prefer) onto your prepared baking sheets. Leave a finger-width space between the strips, as once the mixture is in the oven, it will spread out.

If you prefer to use a spoon, place about ½ teaspoon of the mixture on a prepared baking sheet and use the back of the spoon to spread it into a strip about $\frac{1}{32}$ inch thick. Repeat this step with the rest of the mixture, leaving a finger-width space between the strips. Don't worry about the shape—the mixture will form its own in the oven.

Bake for 10–12 minutes, until the centers of the cookies are pale golden and the edges a darker golden. Remove the baking sheets from the oven, but leave the cookies in place for a few minutes before lifting off with a small, thin spatula and cooling on a wire rack.

4 Puff

The key to baking with puff pastry is to not be scared to let it get dark golden brown so that it is really crispy and the butter inside it takes on a lovely nutty flavor. Pale, soggy puff pastry is always a disappointment.

When you use puff pastry for tarts or something delicate, such as millefeuilles, you need to prick the pastry with a fork in order to deflate some of the air pockets and stop it from rising up too much. It might seem odd to do this after spending so much time creating layers of pastry and air, but even when puff pastry is baked wafer thin and flat, it retains a light flakiness that is completely different from the sweet pastry in the previous chapter.

I hope that you will enjoy making your own puff pastry, but if you don't have the time or the inclination, choose a good ready-made all-butter one.

Makes 12

1 recipe Puff Pastry (see page 44) or 1 pound ready-made all-butter puff pastry

For the béchamel sauce

3½ tablespoons butter

⅓ cup all-purpose flour

1⅔ cups whole milk

sea salt and freshly ground black pepper

freshly grated nutmeg

For the toppings

knob of butter

about 6 large cremini mushrooms, sliced

2 teaspoons chopped parsley

6 slices good-quality pancetta or prosciutto

3.5 ounces Gruyère or Emmentaler cheese, grated

1 egg, beaten with a pinch of salt, for glazing the pastry

Savory slices

A selection of these savory slices, warm from the oven, is great for putting out with coffee in the morning. If you want to make only one flavor, just increase the quantities accordingly. The slices can be made up in their entirety to the point of baking and then frozen. Just defrost them and bake as usual.

Preheat the oven to 400°F and grease two baking sheets.

TO MAKE THE BÉCHAMEL SAUCE: Melt the butter in a heavy-based saucepan over medium heat. When it is bubbling gently, remove from the heat, add the flour, and whisk briskly, until all the butter is absorbed and you have a paste that comes away cleanly from the pan.

Add the milk a little at a time, whisking continuously to avoid lumps. When the milk is all incorporated and the mixture is smooth, put the pan back over medium-low heat, stirring until the sauce starts to bubble. Cook for 1 minute more, then remove from the heat. Season with salt, pepper, and nutmeg, then leave to cool.

TO MAKE THE MUSHROOM TOPPING: Melt the butter in a frying pan, add the mushrooms, and fry gently for a couple minutes, until they color a little. Remove from the heat and stir in the parsley.

Dust your work surface with flour, roll out the pastry ³⁄₁₆ inch thick, then cut into twelve 3-inch squares.

Fold two opposite corners of each square into the middle, then transfer the pastry slices to your prepared baking sheets.

TO MAKE PANCETTA SLICES: Spoon a little sauce onto the pastry where the two corners meet, then add a slice of pancetta and top with a little of the grated cheese.

TO MAKE MUSHROOM SLICES: Mix the mushrooms with one-third of the sauce in a bowl. Spoon some of this mixture onto the pastry where the two corners meet, then top with a little of the grated cheese.

Brush the exposed areas of pastry with the beaten egg and bake in the oven for 12–15 minutes, until golden brown and crispy underneath.

about 9 ounces Spanish chorizo

1 recipe Puff Pastry (see page 44) or 1 pound ready-made all-butter puff pastry

1 egg, beaten with a pinch of salt, for sealing the pastry

Chorizo bites

These circles of pastry with a slice of chorizo inside look like ravioli and are just the right one-mouthful size to serve (warm) with drinks. The easiest way to make them is to seal the slices of chorizo between two strips of pastry and then stamp out the little circles ready for baking. If you want to get ahead, you can make these up to the point of baking and then freeze them. Because they are so small, there is no need to defrost them—just bake as usual, though they may need an extra 5 minutes or so in the oven to ensure they are heated all the way through.

Preheat the oven to 400°F and grease two baking sheets.

Cut the chorizo into 18 slices about ⅜ inch thick.

Dust your work surface with flour, then roll out the pastry into a rectangle measuring about 8 by 6¼ inches. Cut this lengthwise into four equal strips each about 1⅝ inches wide.

Lay two of the strips horizontally in front of you. Place a line of nine chorizo slices along the middle of each strip, leaving ¾ inch between each slice, and a ¾-inch space at either end.

Brush the exposed pastry around the chorizo slices with the beaten egg, then cover with the remaining strips of pastry.

Now you need to seal the pastry around the chorizo. You can do this by pressing delicately with your fingertips. Or, take a small round pastry cutter, just a tiny bit larger than the chorizo, turn it upside down so you are not using the sharp side, then press it very gently around the chorizo to seal the pastry.

Now take a cutter a little larger than the chorizo, and this time use it the right-way up to stamp out nine circles, each with a slice of chorizo in the center. Brush with the beaten egg and, if you like, decorate the top by making little cuts with the tip of a knife (don't cut all the way through the pastry). Repeat for the remaining two strips of pastry and 18 slices of chorizo.

Lay the circles on your prepared baking sheets and bake for about 15 minutes, until the pastry is crispy and golden. Cool for a few minutes before eating.

Makes twelve 3⅛-inch rolls or 24 cocktail-size rolls

For the filling

10 ounces each pork belly, skin removed, and pork shoulder or 1.2 pounds ground pork

1 large onion, finely chopped

1 small bunch curly parsley, finely chopped

scant ½ cup bread crumbs

sea salt and freshly ground black pepper

½ whole nutmeg, grated (or more, to taste)

½ teaspoon ground allspice (or more, to taste)

1 recipe Puff Pastry (see page 44) or 1 pound ready-made all-butter puff pastry

1 egg, beaten with a pinch of salt, for sealing and glazing the pastry

Sausage rolls

Along with quiche, sausage rolls frequently get bad press. Too often they are greasy or stodgy, or filled with bland-tasting sausage meat. But with properly made pastry and a homemade, well-seasoned filling, they are some of the best snack or party foods you can have. You can make them up to the point of baking, then freeze them, ready to defrost and bake as usual. Eat them warm or cold.

I make my sausage meat with half pork belly and half shoulder, which I grind myself, but if you like, you can just buy good-quality ground pork.

Preheat the oven to 400°F and grease a baking sheet.

TO MAKE THE FILLING: If grinding the meat yourself, put through a meat grinder (use the medium-size holes) or use a stand mixer with a medium grinding attachment. Mix the pork with the onion and parsley, then add the bread crumbs and season with salt and pepper and the spices. To test that it is seasoned to your liking, take a little bit of the mixture and fry it in a pan until the meat is cooked through. Taste it and adjust the salt, pepper, and spices as necessary.

Dust your work surface with flour, then roll out the pastry into a rectangle measuring 9½ by 12½ inches and 3/16 inch thick. Cut this lengthwise into three long strips, each about 3⅛ inches wide.

Spoon the sausage meat into a piping bag—a disposable bag is best for this, as you are using raw meat—then pipe a line of it along the length of each strip, just to the right of center. Brush the long, right-hand edge of the pastry with the beaten egg, then fold the opposite edge over to enclose the meat. Press together to seal. Cut widthwise into four pieces if you are making large rolls, or into eight for cocktail rolls. Brush the tops with beaten egg.

Using a knife, score the top of each roll diagonally 6–8 times, but don't cut all the way through the pastry. Place on your prepared baking sheets and bake cocktail-size rolls for 12–15 minutes or larger ones for 18 minutes, until the pastry is golden and crispy. Cool before serving.

Makes one 11-inch tart

1 quantity Puff Pastry (see page 44) or 1 pound ready-
    made all-butter puff pastry

1 recipe Crème Pâtissière (see page 105)

½ recipe Almond Cream (see page 119)

12 apricots

about 1 teaspoon superfine or granulated sugar

about ⅔ cup apricot jam, for glazing (optional)

1–2 tablespoons water (optional)

Apricot tart

This is one of the first classic tarts you are taught how to make as an apprentice baker in France, and you learn the importance of allowing the pastry to become really dark golden brown so that it is properly crisp underneath. The apricot quarters become a little burnt at the tips, giving the tart real character. I still think it is one of the most beautiful of all tarts—crisp pastry, smooth vanilla crème patissière, and the sweet tang of the apricots. It is perfect with no accompaniment whatsoever, except maybe a glass of sweet wine.

If you like, you can make this tart in exactly the same way using plums.

Preheat the oven to 400°F and grease an 11-inch removable-bottomed tart pan or a ring and baking sheet.

Dust your work surface with flour, then roll out the pastry about ³⁄₁₆ inch thick and line your pan or ring set on the prepared baking sheet (see page 34). Prick the base of the pastry with a fork.

Mix together the crème pâtissière and almond cream, then spoon into the pastry crust, spreading it out evenly.

Cut the apricots in half, remove the pits, then cut each half into four wedges, reserving one whole half for the center. Arrange skin side down, in a loose circular fashion on top of the creamy base, pushing one end of each piece gently into the cream, so that the other end points slightly upward. Place the apricot half on top in the center of the tart.

Sprinkle with the sugar. As the tart bakes, it will caramelize on the pointed ends of the apricots, which makes the tart look more attractive.

Place on a baking sheet (if using a tart pan) and bake for 12–15 minutes, then lower the heat to 350°F and bake for a further 20 minutes, until the apricots have caramelized and the pastry is dark golden. If you insert a table knife carefully under the edge of the pastry it should come away from the pan. Leave in the pan for about 15 minutes, then lift out and cool on a rack.

You can leave the tart as it is, but if you want to give the apricots a little sheen, put the apricot jam into a saucepan with the water, and bring to just under a simmer. Don't let the mixture boil or the jam will become too gooey to spread properly. Press the jam through a fine sieve to remove any pulp. Using a pastry brush, lightly glaze the apricots.

Makes two 6¼-inch tarts

For the apple compote

2 large Braeburn apples

1 tablespoon superfine sugar or granulated sugar

splash of brandy

about 1 tablespoon water

1 recipe Puff Pastry (see page 44) or 1 pound ready-made all-butter puff pastry

1 recipe Crème Pâtissière (see page 105)

½ recipe Almond Cream (see page 119)

6 or 7 Braeburn apples

about ⅔ cup apricot jam for glazing

1–2 tablespoons water

Apple tarts

If you are short of time or don't have apples to make the apple purée base for this recipe, you can use a small jar of good-quality applesauce or puréed apple for babies. For the sliced apples, go for a good eating apple, such as Braeburn, or a local or heritage variety that has a good balance of sweetness and sharpness. The tarts are good served either warm or at room temperature.

Preheat the oven to 400°F and grease two 6¼-inch removable-bottomed tart pans or rings and a baking sheet.

TO MAKE THE APPLE COMPOTE: Peel, core, and chop the 2 apples, then put into a saucepan with the sugar, brandy, and water. Simmer until the apples are just soft—about 15 minutes—then blitz to a purée using a blender. Leave to cool.

Dust your work surface with flour, roll out the pastry about ³⁄₁₆ inch thick, and line your pans or rings set on the prepared baking sheet (see page 34). Prick the base of the pastry with a fork.

Mix together the crème pâtissière, almond cream, and apple compote, then spread the mixture inside each pastry crust.

Peel, core, and thinly slice the 6 or 7 apples no more than ¹⁄₁₆ inch thick (see page 203). There are two different ways to arrange the apples: either

place them in overlapping concentric circles, starting from the outer edge, with the rounded edges facing outward, or simply overlap them in one circle like a pinwheel, then arrange a few slices in a rosette in the center.

Place on a baking sheet (if using tart pans) and bake for 30–40 minutes, or until both the apples and pastry are golden brown and the tips of the apples are dark brown. The base of the tarts should be crispy. If baked in a ring, you should be able to lift them without sticking from the baking sheet with a large spatula.

Put the apricot jam into a saucepan with the water and bring to just under a simmer. Don't let the mixture boil or the jam will become too gooey to spread properly. Press the jam through a fine sieve to remove any pulp. Using a pastry brush, lightly glaze the top of each tart. Eat warm or at room temperature.

Makes one 9-inch tart

1 recipe Puff Pastry (see page 44) or 1 pound ready-made all-butter puff pastry

6–8 Braeburn or other good baking apples

7 tablespoons butter

1 cup superfine sugar

pinch of ground cinnamon

Tarte Tatin

I'm sure everyone knows the story of how this tart is supposed to have been created accidentally by *les demoiselles* Tatin—the Tatin sisters—but in case you haven't . . . One of the sisters is said to have been softening apples in butter and sugar for an apple tart, then realized that she had left them in too long so they had caramelized and were sticking to the pan. She tried to rescue the situation by putting the pastry over the top, popping the pan into the oven, then turning the whole thing over to serve it. The guests at the hotel where the sisters worked apparently loved it. Whether the story is true or not, the tart has become one of the most famous French desserts.

There is an assumption that tarte Tatin is difficult to make, but when I teach people how to do it, they usually find that the only tricky part is turning the tart over when it has been baked. I think it helps to make it in a frying pan rather than in a pan because you can hold on to the handle to turn it over.

There are various schools of thought about how to make the tart. Some people slice the apples; others halve them, which is the way I prefer. Some people fill the pan with sugar then put in the apples, cover them with pastry, and put the pan into the oven straightaway, but this way you run the risk of the sugar becoming only a light, rather anemic-looking caramel. I prefer something a bit darker and more toffee-like, so I start the tart off on the stove to get the caramel going. The key is to do this slowly and carefully so that the sugar doesn't get too dark, or even burn, and become brittle—more like a candy apple than tarte Tatin, and not good for the teeth.

Choose an apple that has a good balance of sweetness and sharpness, such as Braeburn, or one of the characterful local or heritage varieties you can often find in farmers' markets.

(Continued)

Preheat the oven to 400°F.

Dust your work surface with flour and roll out the pastry until it is about ³⁄₁₆ inch thick and large enough to fit loosely in a 9-inch ovenproof frying pan. Prick the pastry well all over and either lay it on a large plate or place a sheet of waxed paper over the top and roll it up, then put it into the refrigerator to rest while you prepare the apples and sugar.

Peel the apples, then cut in half from top to bottom and remove the cores.

Melt the butter in the frying pan over medium heat. Sprinkle the sugar and cinnamon over it and cook gently for about 1 minute. Quickly arrange the apples, cut side up, in the pan and keep over medium heat, shaking the pan from time to time to ensure that the apples don't stick to the bottom. Don't worry if you can't fit in all the apples initially; they will shrink a little as they cook and you will be able to squeeze in more as necessary. You need to pack the apples together tightly so that the tart holds its shape when you turn it over.

Continue cooking gently and shaking the pan until the sugar turns to a rich caramel—this will take about 30 minutes. Remove the pan from the heat and rest it for 5 minutes.

Remove the pastry from the refrigerator and lay it loosely over the top of the apples. It needs to be tucked in around the edge of the pan until it almost touches the caramel. The best way to do this without your fingers touching the caramel, which burns very badly, is to use the back of a teaspoon to nudge the pastry into place.

Bake for about 30 minutes, until the pastry is really dark golden brown. Don't forget that when you flip the tart over after it is baked, the pastry is going to be the base holding the apples and caramel together, so it needs to be really well colored and crispy, otherwise it will become soggy with the juices from the apples.

Remove the pan from the oven and leave to cool for about 1 minute. This lets the caramel set a little and also makes it safer to turn out, but take care as the caramel will still be hot.

Place a large plate over the pan and, holding both plate and pan firmly, turn them over together so that the tart is apple side up on the plate. You can serve the tart at room temperature, but I think it is best warm, with crème fraîche or vanilla ice cream.

Variation

For a little twist to the classic recipe, I suggest you use a butter flavored with sea salt. It will give a gorgeous salted caramel flavor to the tart.

1 recipe Puff Pastry (see page 44) or 1 pound ready-made all-butter puff pastry, cut in half

1 recipe Almond Cream (see page 119)

1 dried or ceramic bean (optional), to put inside the tart

1 egg, beaten with a pinch of salt, for glazing the pastry

½ cup superfine sugar or 1 tablespoon confectioners' sugar

7 tablespoons water (optional)

Galette des rois

The feast of Epiphany (January 6) is a special day in France and is often marked by baking this traditional "kings' cake," named after the Three Kings. It is very simple: frangipane (almond cream) sandwiched between two rounds of puff pastry, with a dried (or ceramic) bean inside. Whoever gets the slice with the bean is king (or queen) for the day. Nowadays, you can buy all sorts of porcelain figurines to put inside the cake instead of the bean. You just have to warn everyone to look out for something hard so they don't break their teeth. In some families, the tradition is that whoever is the king gets to choose the queen, or vice versa. In our family, we used to have two cakes: a kings' cake and a queens' cake, with a bean inside each one. It was more democratic!

Preheat the oven to 400°F and grease a baking sheet.

Dust your work surface with flour and roll each piece of pastry into a circle about 3/16 inch thick and 8 inches in diameter. The exact size doesn't matter too much as long as the circles are the same.

With a blunt knife, mark a border all the way around one circle about 3/16 inch in from the edge without cutting all the way through the pastry; alternatively, press the blunt side of a smaller-size cutter lightly into the pastry. Prick the area of pastry inside the border with a fork. By doing this, you will stop the central area from puffing up too much while letting the outer edge rise up to form a rim.

(Continued)

Lift the pastry base onto your prepared baking sheet and spread the almond cream over the pricked area. If you like, hide the bean somewhere inside the cream.

Brush the pastry rim with the beaten egg, then lay the other circle of pastry on top. With your fingertips, press gently from the center outward to remove any air pockets, then press the edges of the two circles together. With the back of a knife, decorate the top in a crisscross pattern, then go around the edge, pushing the back of the knife into the pastry at intervals to give a scalloped effect.

Brush the top of the galette with two coats of beaten egg, then use your knife to make a small hole in the top of the pastry to allow steam to escape. Bake for about 25 minutes, reducing the heat to 350°F halfway through the baking time. The pastry should be dark golden.

To finish the galette, you can glaze it in one of two ways. Put the superfine sugar in a saucepan with the water, bring to a boil, then reduce the heat and simmer briefly until you have a light syrup. Brush this all over the top of the galette and leave to cool. Alternatively, dust the top with the confectioners' sugar and put the galette back into the oven just long enough for the sugar to melt and form a shiny glaze. Leave to cool before eating.

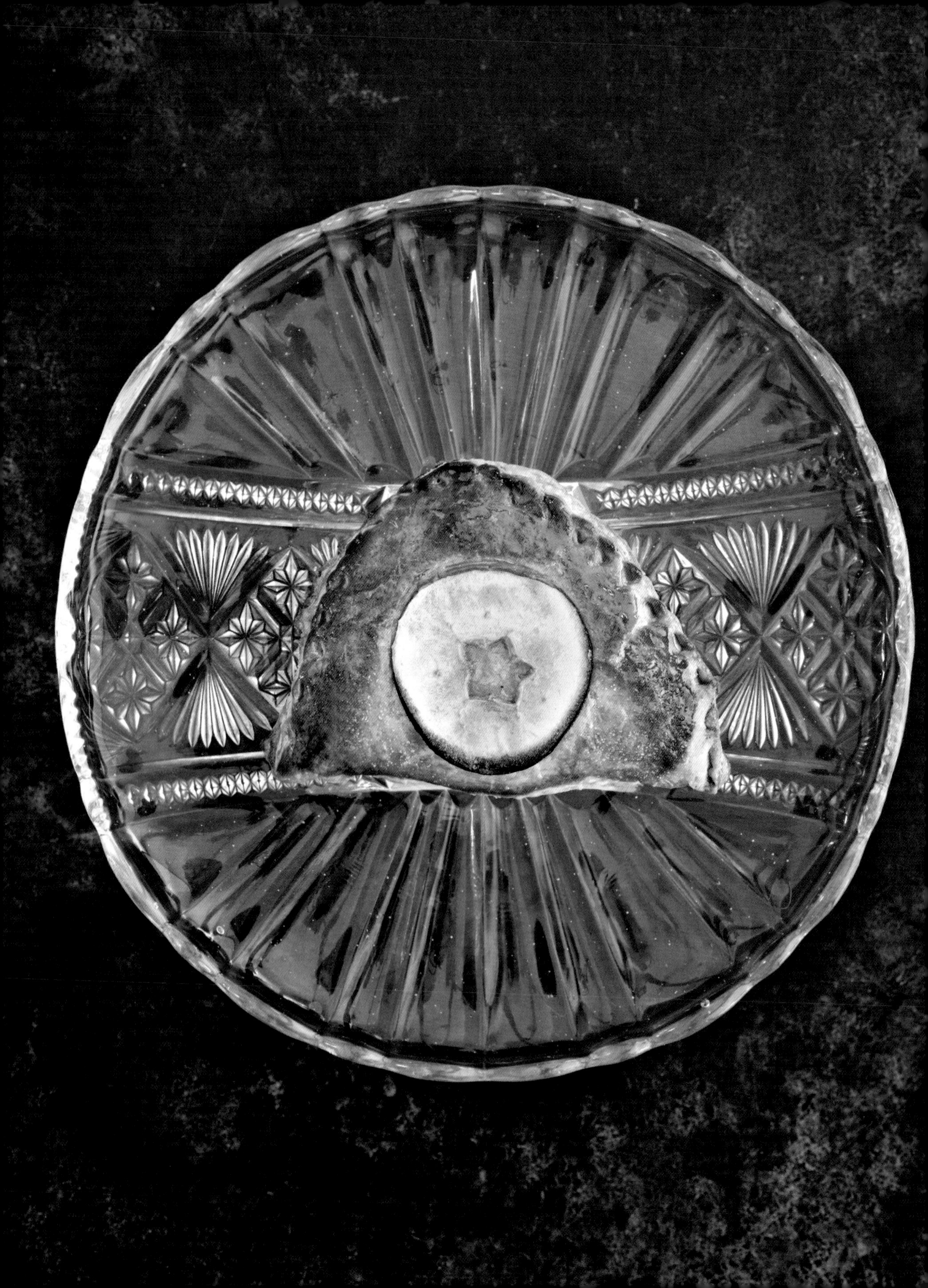

Makes 12

½ recipe Crème Pâtissière (see page 105) or Crème
Légère (see page 211)

½ recipe Almond Cream (see page 119)

½ recipe Apple Compote (see page 161)

1 recipe Puff Pastry (see page 44) or 1 pound ready-made
all-butter puff pastry

1 egg, beaten with a pinch of salt, for sealing the pastry

1 large apple, such as Braeburn, or 2 small ones

superfine sugar, for sprinkling

Apple & custard "leftovers"

In France, these pastries are known as *chaussons aux pommes*. *Chaussons* are slippers, the kind of cozy slip-ons that are associated with granddads, and their apple namesakes are great comfort food. In England, the usual name for these pastries is "turnovers," but I call them "leftovers" because they are a great way of using up any puff pastry, crème pâtissière, almond cream, or apple compote that is left after you have made some of the other recipes in this book. When I was an apprentice in France, we never wasted anything, and used to mix up all three creams, as they make a fantastic combination. However, if you don't have them all, you could combine just two, or even use them alone. Whatever filling is used, you will need around 1 pound (roughly 2 cups) of it to one recipe of pastry.

The filled pastries can be frozen, ready to be defrosted and baked in the usual way when you need them.

Preheat the oven to 400°F and grease two baking sheets.

Mix together the crème pâtissière, almond cream, and apple compote in a bowl.

Dust your work surface with flour and roll out the pastry ³⁄₁₆ inch thick. Using a cutter about 4 inches in diameter or a plate and a knife, cut out 12 circles.

Brush the edges with the beaten egg, then spoon some of the cream mixture into the middle of each circle. Fold the pastry over itself to form a half-moon shape, then press the edges together and crimp with a fork. Leaving the skin on the apple(s), slice very thinly widthwise through the core, so that you end up with 12 rings about ¹⁄₁₆ inch thick. Push out the seeds, which will leave each slice with a star-shaped hole in the center.

Brush each "leftover" with beaten egg and lay a slice of apple on top. Sprinkle with a little superfine sugar, then place on your prepared baking sheets and bake for 20 minutes, until the base of each pastry is golden brown.

Makes 5 slices

1 recipe Puff Pastry (see page 44) or 1 pound ready-made all-butter puff pastry

a little rum

1 recipe Crème Pâtissière (see page 105) or Crème Légère (see page 211)

confectioners' sugar, for dusting

Millefeuilles

The name of these means "1,000 leaves," which is simply a way of describing this classic light dessert, with its multilayered pastry sandwiching layers of creamy filling. Millefeuille is one of the first things that would-be pastry chefs are taught at college, and the key is to get the right balance of pastry and filling. Too much of one or the other and you don't get the full, mouth-filling pleasure of the contrasting textures and flavors. Often I see mass-produced millefeuilles made with pale-looking, uninteresting pastry, overfilled with artificial-tasting cream, and smothered in colored icing. I like to keep millefeuilles simple, elegant, and classic, filled only with crème pâtissière or crème légère.

Preheat the oven to 400°F and grease a baking sheet.

Dust your work surface with flour, roll out the pastry into a rectangle measuring 12 by 8 inches and about 3/16 inch thick. Place on your prepared baking sheet and prick well all over with a fork. Bake for about 20 minutes, until golden, then turn over very carefully, place a similar-size baking sheet on top to keep the pastry from rising, and return to the oven for 5–10 minutes, until golden brown. Remove and cool on a rack.

When cool, cut the pastry rectangle widthwise into three strips, each about 4 inches wide. You will see that each strip has a flat side and a more bobbly side. Reserve the strip with the best flat side for the top. Of the other strips, lay one of them with the flat side facing down on your work surface. Mix the rum into the crème pâtissière and spoon half of this down the center (alternatively, you can pipe it; see page 61). Don't spread it, or it will ooze out once you put the pastry on top. Instead, just place the next strip of pastry on top, again flat side down, and press it down very gently. Spoon or pipe the rest of the cream as before, then top with your reserved strip of pastry; this time you want the flat side facing upward.

Sift confectioners' sugar over the top until completely covered. Then, if you like, take two metal skewers and put one over a lit gas burner to heat. Use the hot skewer to carefully and lightly brand the sugar diagonally in one direction. While you are doing this, heat the second skewer and use it to do the same thing in the opposite direction so that you create a dark crisscross pattern in the sugar. If you don't have a gas burner, you could use a blowtorch to heat the skewers. If you don't have either, leave the confectioners' sugar as it is.

Finally, with a sharp knife, carefully cut widthwise into five slices, washing and drying the knife after each cut so that you keep the slices looking neat.

Makes 12

confectioners' sugar, for dusting

1 recipe Puff Pastry (see page 44) or 1 pound ready-made all-butter puff pastry

1 recipe Crème Pâtissière (see page 105)

ground cinnamon or freshly grated nutmeg (optional)

Natas (Portuguese custard tarts)

When I first came to London, I lived near Portobello Road, and it was always a treat to go to the Lisboa Pâtisserie for one of their famous and gorgeous Portuguese tarts. I say "one," but the problem was you always wanted more.

Although I have called them custard tarts, I make my *natas* with crème pâtissière rather than custard (crème anglaise), which is baked until you get dark brown patches on top.

In France, I had grown up eating *flan*, which is a similar kind of tart, but usually a big one cut into slices. The little, deep, and irregular-shaped *natas* have a greater ratio of pastry to custard, and because you roll the pastry in sugar, it becomes caramelized in places: irresistible! You can finish the tarts with a sprinkling of cinnamon or nutmeg if you like, though I prefer them plain.

Lightly grease a 12-hole miniature muffin pan. Even if you use a nonstick pan—unless it is brand new—it is worth doing this as the sugar on the pastry will caramelize and cling to any bits of the pan that have lost their nonstick properties.

Dust your work surface with confectioners' sugar. Remove the pastry from the refrigerator and roll it out about ³⁄₁₆ inch thick, sprinkling well with more confectioners' sugar as you go.

Use a pastry cutter to cut 12 rounds of pastry about 4 inches in diameter; they need to be big enough to line the holes and leave a little overhang (see page 35). Put the pan into the refrigerator to rest for about 1 hour.

Preheat the oven to 400°F.

Remove the pan from the refrigerator and fill each pastry crust with crème pâtissière. Sprinkle with cinnamon or nutmeg (if using). Bake for 15–20 minutes, until the pastry is golden, the sugar it was rolled in is caramelized, and the crème pâtissière is dark in spots. Allow to cool for just a few minutes before lifting the tarts out of the pan; don't leave them in much longer, or the caramelized sugar may weld the tarts to the pan. Leave to cool completely before eating.

Makes 8

superfine sugar or granulated sugar, for sprinkling or dusting

1 recipe Puff Pastry (see page 44) or 1 pound ready-made all-butter puff pastry

ground cinnamon, for sprinkling (optional)

Palmiers

Traditionally, these French pastries are shaped like a palm leaf or a butterfly, but mine are more freestyle and quite fun to make. Kids love doing them, and though, in my experience, the palmiers are usually gone the minute they have cooled down, they will keep in an airtight container for 3–4 days.

Preheat the oven to 350°F and grease a baking sheet.

Sprinkle or dust your work surface with sugar and roll out the puff pastry until you have a square or rectangle about 3⁄16 inch thick. Cut it into 24 squares measuring 2–2½ inches.

Sprinkle each square with a little sugar and with cinnamon, if you like, then set three squares on top of one another so that you have eight little stacks. Sprinkle more sugar on top of each stack, then take a wooden spoon and press the length of the handle down diagonally across the top of each stack so that it sinks in the center and the edges lift up.

Place the palmiers on the prepared baking sheet and bake for 10–15 minutes, until golden and caramelized. They will puff up in different ways, so they are quite quirky. Cool on a wire rack for 5 minutes.

½ recipe Puff Pastry (see page 44) or 8 ounces ready-made all-butter puff pastry

1 cup confectioners' sugar

about 1 cup sliced almonds or ground pistachios or a few tablespoons sesame seeds or poppy seeds,
   or some of each

Croustillants

These are wafer-thin slices of puff pastry, coated in sugar, and baked so that they are crunchy (*croustillant* is French for something crispy), and they are perfect for using up scraps of puff pastry left over from making tarts, sausage rolls, or the like. You can sandwich them together with chantilly cream (see page 181) and berries, or any fruit you like, to make a smart-looking dessert. However, I also like to encrust them in nuts or seeds, as in this recipe, to make simpler cookies. Because any humidity in the air will affect their crispiness, croustillants are best made and eaten within a few hours.

Preheat the oven to 400°F and line two baking sheets with parchment paper.

Roll the puff pastry into a sausage shape about 9½ inches long, then cut into 24 slices about ⅜ inch thick.

Dust your work surface with some of the confectioners' sugar and place a piece of pastry on it, cut side down. Sprinkle a little more sugar on top and, using a small rolling pin, roll the pastry into a long, roughly oval shape that is paper-thin.

Turn it over several times while rolling to coat it in the sugar and to make sure that it doesn't stick. Repeat with the remaining pieces of pastry, adding more sugar as needed.

Lay the croustillants on the prepared baking sheets and sprinkle the top of each with your chosen nuts or seeds—about 1 teaspoon per croustillant. Bake for 6–8 minutes, until the croustillants are caramelized. Be sure to keep a close eye on them as they can burn quickly. Use a thin spatula to lift them from the baking sheets and cool on a wire rack.

5 Choux

Choux pastry is less of a dough, more of a batter, that is very easy to make and is used for all kinds of light savory buns and sweet confections, such as cream puffs, profiteroles, and éclairs. The moisture in the batter causes it to expand in the heat of the oven, and this creates a pastry that is hollow inside. Once it has cooled down, you can inject the cavity with anything from cream cheese and smoked salmon to sweet chantilly cream or crème pâtissière. Sweet buns are often glazed with chocolate (as in éclairs and profiteroles) or stacked up in a pyramid and drizzled with chocolate sauce, or swirled in spun sugar to make the classic French wedding cake, *croquembouche*.

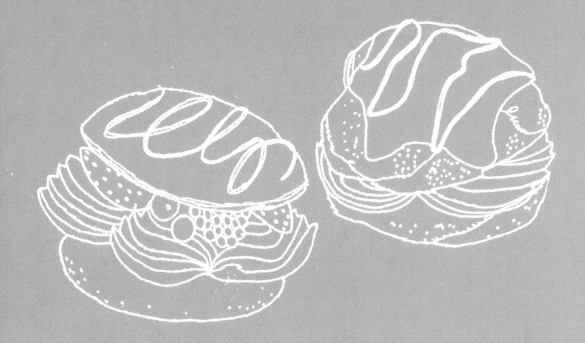

There are two skills involved in making successful choux pastry. The first is becoming confident at using a piping bag so that you can create the shapes you want, from round buns to long, elegant éclairs, or the necks and bodies that can be assembled to make choux swans. The second skill is baking the pastry properly so that it not only puffs up, but also dries out, which means that when you take it from the oven, it doesn't deflate and become limp, but provides a strong support for whatever you are going to pipe inside it.

Some people put sugar into the choux batter if it is going to be filled with cream or glazed with melted chocolate, but I prefer not to add sugar because it tends to prevent the pastry from drying out well. Instead, I have just the one recipe for choux pastry, and it works for both savory and sweet fillings.

Makes 12

1 recipe Choux Pastry (see page 56)

1 egg, beaten with a pinch of salt, for glazing

For the chantilly cream

1 cup heavy cream

2 tablespoons superfine sugar

a few drops of vanilla extract or rose water (optional)

confectioners' sugar, for dusting

Swans

Yes, I know these are very 1970s, but we include them in the classes at our school because they offer a great way to become used to piping choux pastry, and people are fascinated to see how they are assembled, and very proud of themselves when they have made them.

The swan necks are the trickiest part because they are very delicate and fragile, which is why I suggest you pipe double the quantity you need, as up to half of them are likely to break when you lift them off your baking sheet or silicone mat. Casualties are just a hazard of swan making.

I use three different fabric piping bags for these. Two are filled with choux batter for piping the necks and bodies of the swans: one bag has a thin tip and the other a medium star-shaped tip. The third bag I use to pipe the chantilly cream, again with a medium star-shaped tip. You need three bags ready to go, as there is no time to wash and dry them between piping, but you can, of course, use disposable bags.

The chantilly cream that forms the swans' feathers is also good for serving with fruit tarts.

(Continued)

 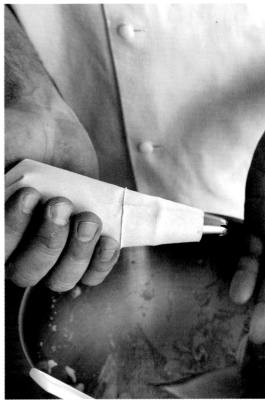

Preheat the oven to 325°F. Lightly grease two nonstick baking sheets or line them with silicone mats.

Prepare three piping bags: insert ⅜-inch star tips into two of them and a plain tip with a tiny hole the size of a ballpoint pen into the third.

Take two piping bags—the one with the fine plain tip and one with a star tip—and fill with batter (see page 61).

To pipe, hold the bag in one hand with the other hand underneath to steady and guide it. Squeeze with the hand holding the bag, pipe, then turn the bag counterclockwise, squeeze again, applying the same pressure all the time, and pipe again. I have noticed that most people tend to hold the bag with one hand and squeeze with the other, but this doesn't give you the same control.

First make the swans' necks. Using the bag with the fine tip, pipe 24 thin S shapes onto a prepared baking sheet.

Now change to the bag with the star tip and pipe the bodies onto the second prepared baking sheet. Squeezing gently, pipe a rosette shape, then draw the bag toward you so that you end up with an elongated body with a little tail. Repeat until you have 12 bodies.

(Continued)

Put the baking sheet containing the necks into the oven and bake for 8–10 minutes, checking all the time to make sure they don't burn. They should be golden brown, but will go from beautifully golden to burnt very quickly if you don't keep an eye on them. Remove the baking sheet from the oven and leave to cool.

Brush the tops of the bodies very lightly with the beaten egg—not so much that it drips onto the baking sheet. The bodies need to bake longer than the necks in order to dry out properly. They should take about 20 minutes, by which time they will be golden and puffed up. For the last 4 minutes of baking, leave the oven door slightly ajar to allow the steam to escape and help the drying process. Remove the baking sheet from the oven and leave to cool.

(Continued)

TO MAKE THE CHANTILLY CREAM: Whisk the cream, sugar, and vanilla together until thick. Be careful not to overwhisk or you will end up with butter rather than cream. Fill your third piping bag with the mixture.

Slice the top off each choux pastry body—the inside should be dry and hollow. Lay the tops, cut side down, on your work surface and cut in half to make "wings."

Using a circular motion, pipe some of the cream into the cavity of each body. Gently insert a wing (shiny side up) into the cream on each side.

With a scraper or small, thin spatula, carefully lift each swan neck from the baking sheet and insert into the cream at the opposite end to the tail. Finally, very lightly dust the whole swan with a tiny amount of confectioners' sugar.

1 recipe Choux Pastry (see page 56)

1 recipe Chantilly Cream (see page 181)

7 ounces good-quality milk or dark chocolate (optional)

Chocolate éclairs

Éclairs are made in much the same way as the swans on page 181 but are a lot simpler, as you only need to pipe the choux pastry in straight lines.

The chocolate glaze is simply made by melting good chocolate. Unless you like a bitter edge to the flavor, you don't need a chocolate with a very high percentage of cacao: 53 percent is fine.

Although I suggest chantilly cream for the filling as it is quite light and fluffy, you could also use crème pâtissière (see page 105). A classic bakery filling is crème pâtissière with a good dash of rum mixed into it. Or, you could use Chocolate Créme Pâtissière (page 208) or Coffee Crème Pâtissière (page 209).

Preheat the oven to 325°F. Lightly grease a nonstick baking sheet or line it with a silicone mat.

Fit a piping bag with a plain tip about ⅜ inch in diameter and fill with the choux batter (see page 61).

If making large éclairs, pipe 12 lines 5–6 inches long onto your prepared baking sheet. If making small éclairs, pipe 24 lines about 3¼ inches long.

Bake large éclairs for 15–20 minutes, and small ones for 12–15 minutes, until golden and puffed up. For the last 4 minutes of baking, leave the oven door slightly ajar to allow the steam to escape and help the drying process. Remove the baking sheet from the oven and leave to cool.

There are two ways to fill the éclairs with the cream. You can either carefully cut them in half lengthwise and pipe the cream inside using a piping bag with a medium-size star tip (about ⅜ inch in diameter), or you can make a small hole at each end of each éclair and squeeze cream into the hollow using a piping bag with a plain tip (about ³⁄₁₆ inch in diameter).

If you want to glaze the éclairs with chocolate, it needs to be done at different times, depending on which method of filling you are using. If you are planning to cut the éclairs in half and fill them with cream, dip the top halves in chocolate before filling them. If injecting the éclair filling, inject them first and then dip the éclairs in chocolate; otherwise, you can do it after you have injected the cream.

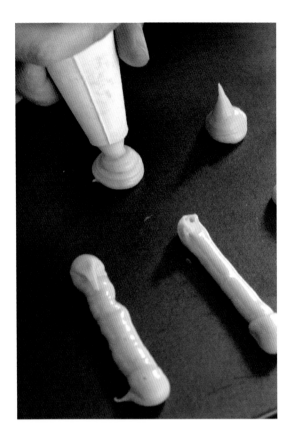

Break the chocolate into chunks and put into a heatproof bowl. Place this over a pan of simmering water—you need enough water to come close to the bottom of the bowl but not actually touch it. Turn the heat very low so that you don't get steam into the bowl, as this can make the chocolate stiffen and look dull. Let the chocolate melt slowly, stirring all the time. Remove from the heat.

If you are halving the éclairs, take the upper halves one by one and dip the tops into the chocolate. Let the excess drain off into the bowl, then place on a wire rack until the chocolate has set. You can then pipe the cream into the cavities of the bottom halves and put the chocolate-dipped halves on top. If you are injecting cream inside the éclairs, you can do this before dipping them in the chocolate. Again, leave them on a rack until the chocolate sets.

Variation

You could also make the éclairs without the chocolate glaze on top and simply halve and fill them with chantilly cream and fresh fruit. If you want to do this, lightly glaze the top of the unbaked strips with 1 egg beaten with a pinch of salt, and run the tines of a fork along it for decoration before baking. When the éclairs are filled, dust with confectioners' sugar.

Makes 24

1 recipe Choux Pastry (see page 56)

1 egg, beaten with a pinch of salt, for glazing

8–10 brown sugar cubes, coarsely crushed, or about ⅓ cup chopped skinned hazelnuts,
    or use half quantities of each, mixed together

Chouquettes

These are little buns topped with crushed sugar and/or chopped hazelnuts (see photo on pages 190–191). Because they are baked for quite a short length of time, they are slightly soft and chewy. If you like, though, you can leave them in the oven for a little longer in order to dry them out a bit more and keep them firmly puffed up. Then you can fill them with chantilly cream (see page 181) or crème pâtissière (see page 105). A great thing to do for a party is to arrange them in a pyramid on a big plate, melt some chocolate (see page 189), and spoon it over the top.

Preheat the oven to 325°F. Lightly grease a nonstick baking sheet or line it with a silicone mat.

Fit a piping bag with a plain tip about ⅜ inch in diameter and fill with the choux batter (see page 61).

Pipe twenty-four 1-inch-diameter dots onto the prepared baking sheet (see photo on page 189). Brush the tops very lightly with the beaten egg and sprinkle with the crushed sugar.

Bake for 12–15 minutes, until golden and puffed. For the last 4 minutes of baking, leave the oven door slightly ajar to allow the steam to escape and help the drying process. Remove the baking sheet from the oven and leave to cool.

Makes 24–30

vegetable oil, for deep-frying

1 recipe Choux Pastry (see page 56)

scant 1 cup grated good strong Cheddar or Gruyère cheese

smoked paprika, for dusting

Cheese puffs

You can bake these in the same way as Chouquettes (see facing page), but I like them best walnut size and deep-fried, then dusted with smoked paprika—great for serving with drinks.

Put some vegetable oil in a deep-fryer or deep pan (making sure it comes no further than a third of the way up) and heat to 325°F. (If you don't have a thermometer, you can test if the oil is hot enough by dropping in a little of the choux mixture—it should sizzle.)

Using a teaspoon, take walnut-size pieces of the batter and ease them into the oil. Fry for 2–3 minutes, until puffed up and golden. Lift out with a slotted spoon, drain on paper towels, and dust with smoked paprika.

Makes about 12

8.9 ounces all-purpose flour	250 g
½ teaspoon baking powder	
1.7 ounces butter	50 g
1 teaspoon salt	
0.7 ounce granulated sugar	20 g
8.9 ounces water	250 g
vegetable oil, for deep-frying	
superfine sugar, for dusting	

Churros

This is my final bonus recipe, which is made in a slightly different way from the basic choux pastry. In fact, it is rather like a variation on the hot-water crust recipe on page 85, but I just had to include it because I love churros. In Spain, if you try to walk past one of the cafés that specializes in these strips of sugary doughnut, the smell of hot oil and sugar is just impossible to resist.

Traditionally, they are made using a *churrera*, a pump with a special nozzle that squeezes the churro mixture into hot oil in long, snaking, ridged rings. Once these are fried, they are snipped into short lengths and dusted in sugar and sometimes cinnamon, ready for dipping into the thick hot chocolate that is usually served with them. At home you can use a piping bag and snip the mixture into shorter, more manageable lengths as you pipe it into the oil. The secret is to fry them slowly at a relatively low temperature so that they get crispy on the outside, without burning, and are well cooked all the way through, otherwise they can be stodgy.

Put the flour and baking powder into a bowl.

Put the butter, salt, and sugar into a saucepan with the water. Bring to a boil and boil for 1 minute, then pour the mixture into the flour bowl, beating well until you have a thick batter.

Fit a piping bag with a large star tip about ⅝ inch in diameter and fill with the batter (see page 182).

Put some vegetable oil in a deep-fryer or deep saucepan (making sure it comes no further than a third of the way up) and heat to 325°F. (If you don't have a thermometer, you can test if the oil is hot enough by dropping in a little of the mixture—it should sizzle.)

With one hand, pipe the mixture into the oil, using the other hand to snip it off every 5 inches or so with a pair of kitchen scissors. Fry for 3–4 minutes, turning over regularly until the churros are golden on all sides. Lift out and drain briefly on paper towels.

Put some superfine sugar on a large plate. While the churros are still hot, toss them in the sugar.

Variation

Instead of serving hot chocolate for dipping the churros into, you could make a sauce with 3.5 ounces melted dark chocolate (see page 189) mixed with 2 tablespoons heavy cream.

6   Finishing Touches

I am often asked how to present fruit tarts so that they look as artistic as the ones people have seen in the windows of pastry shops and bakeries when they are on vacation in France. Well, the secret is really in the cutting of the fruit as much as the arrangement, so here are a few tricks and tips.

Strawberries

In a classic strawberry tart, the fruit is laid on top of a chantilly cream filling (see page 181) or crème pâtissière (see page 105). Make sure the berries are firm but ripe: remember, flavor is more important than appearance. Try to keep the size of your fruit in proportion with your tart(s): choose small berries for little tartlets. If you have tiny berries, or are using wild strawberries, which are usually very small, you can stand them upright, packing them close together. For little round tarts, begin with one upright strawberry in the center, then pack the other berries around it, upright and in circles, working outward. For little square tarts, you can arrange a line of upright berries along each side to make a border, then place the rest in upright lines within that.

For larger tarts, use bigger berries and cut them in half. If you are using just a few whole, halved, or sliced strawberries on a mixed fruit tart, it can look more eye-catching if you leave the stems and leafy hulls attached. But if you are topping a tart only with strawberries, this can be a bit much, so remove them—carefully. If you tug at the stem clumsily, the hull will come away, leaving a jagged hole, and the strawberries will end up looking like they have had a bite taken out of them. If necessary, use the point of a vegetable peeler or a pair of tweezers to help you remove the hulls cleanly.

When you stand a strawberry upright with the hull at the top, you will see that it looks more bulbous at the top end, so if you are halving or slicing the fruit, cut lengthwise from top to bottom to get the best, most rounded heart shape.

If you are using only strawberries on a large tart, start the arrangement in the middle of the tart with one halved berry, cut side down, then work outward in circles. Imagine you are tiling a roof and that the strawberry halves are tiles. Lay them cut side down and pointed ends toward the center, slightly overlapping, round and round so that there are no gaps through which you can see the filling underneath.

Raspberries

As with strawberries, choose berries that are firm but ripe, and, if you like, combine yellow and white varieties with red ones. Keep raspberries whole and upright, with the tip (rather than the hollow end) pointing upward. If you are making a square tart, arrange the berries in rows. If you are making a round tart, start in the center (as with strawberries), then work outward in circles, packing the berries tightly together to hide the filling beneath. Alternatively, if you want a really dense, compact layer of raspberries, lay the berries on their sides rather than standing them up, and push the tip of one into the hollow of the next so that they join together.

Stone Fruit

Fruits such as peaches and nectarines tend to be used freshly sliced on a cream filling or crème pâtissière base, whereas apricots and plums, once arranged on a tart, are often baked. Sometimes they are even poached whole in order to soften their texture before they are sliced. On a large tart, apricots or plums look impressive cut into quarters and arranged with the tips pointing upward so that these blacken a little during baking and give definition to the pattern of fruit.

If you are slicing stone fruits, leave the skin on and cut in half before removing the pit. Provided the fruit is ripe, the pit should come out cleanly. Slice each half of the fruit thinly with a sharp knife, making half-moon shapes about ¹⁄₁₆ inch thick. These look most effective on round tarts because you can make a rose pattern with the slices of fruit. Start at the outer edge and, using the largest slices first, arrange them with the skin side facing upward so that they overlap one another. Then work inward, continuing to overlap the slices in concentric circles, and gradually moving on to the smaller slices. Keep a few of the very smallest for the center and, when you reach it, arrange two, three, or four slices (depending on the size of the tart), tightly overlapping each other, leaving just a small space in the very center for the last slice. Curl this tightly around itself and place it upright in this space, so that it resembles the heart of a rose.

Apples

The key to producing neat-looking apple slices is to peel the fruit starting at the stem end and go around the circumference. This will give you a nice rounded shape that can be sliced into neat half-moons. Peeling the fruit in strips from stem to base might seem easier, but this gives a flatter, less rounded shape and produces angular slices.

The secret to successful peeling is to hold the peeler still and move the apple, not the other way around. In my classes, people often get quite competitive about trying to take all the peel off in one strip—and I admit when I was an apprentice we used to do the same thing in the bakery—but it really doesn't matter if it takes one go or several.

Once the apples are peeled, use a small, sharp knife to cut each one in half and take out the core as neatly and sparingly as possibly. Try not to make a crater around it, as that is just a waste of apple.

Next, to slice your apple neatly and efficiently, put each half, flat side down, on your work surface, with the cavity where the core used to be running from left to right. Slice downward all the way across the apple half, keeping your cuts about ³⁄₁₆ inch apart.

If you are making round tarts, arrange the apples either in circles or in a rose pattern (as for stone fruit, see facing page).

Mixed Fresh Fruit Tarts

This is a chance to experiment and have fun on a chantilly cream filling (page 181) or crème pâtissière base, mixing fruits such as kiwi and red or white currants with the more classical tart fruits such as berries and apricots.

Some people like to add a few rounds of banana. If you do this, be aware that the cut fruit will darken very quickly, so squeeze a little lemon juice over it. Also, if you are glazing the fruit with apricot jam (see facing page), make sure you cover the banana really well with it to prevent any discoloration.

Peel kiwi fruits neatly with a peeler, then slice into rounds, or cut in half lengthwise before slicing so that you have half-moon shapes.

If you are using oranges, separate them into segments, but don't peel away the membrane or cut them, as they will lose too much juice and begin to look dry very quickly.

Of course, you could keep each fruit separate, in lines or circles, but it is quite difficult to make fruits of different sizes and shapes look neat, so I prefer a looser approach. The important thing is to get some height, so I like to put in a few small bunches of red or white currants, and mix whole berries with slices of other fruits.

Usually, I begin by making a border all the way around, with overlapping slices of nectarines or peaches. Next, I might arrange some slices of kiwi and halved strawberries on top of the stone fruit, at intervals around the outside. If I am making a square tart, I would probably mark each corner with a halved strawberry and each side with a slice of kiwi. Although I don't normally recommend arranging strawberries cut side up as they dry out quickly, they can look good, one in each corner, or dotted around the edge of a round tart, with the green hull left on and facing outward. Once I have placed fruit around the borders, I will just make a "picture" with the remaining fruit, packing it in to create a combination of different colors, heights, and shapes. I find that the looser and less neat you try to be, the better.

Glazing

Glaze fresh fruits with melted apricot jam (see page 105), warmed and pressed through a fine sieve to remove any pulp, to give the tart a professional-looking finish and sheen. The secret is just to melt the jam in a saucepan with 1–2 tablespoons water, but don't let it boil or it will become gluey. Holding the pan with one hand and a wide brush in the other, dab the glaze onto the fruit gently and neatly; don't drag the brush or you will disturb the fruit. As the glaze cools, it will thicken again, so don't persevere with it or you will end up with lumps and dollops, which will ruin the look of your tart. Just put the pan back on the heat and warm up the glaze again so that you keep it fluid all the time.

Alternative Creams

Half the fun of making tarts is experimenting, not only with different fruits, colors, and textures, but also with the flavors of the creams that you use as a filling base. Following are a few ideas.

Note: In all these creams, low-fat milk could be used instead of whole milk if you prefer, but the end result will not be as rich.

Makes about 1⅔ cups

1 cup whole milk

1 vanilla bean

4½ tablespoons superfine sugar

2 teaspoons unsweetened cocoa powder

3 egg yolks

3½ tablespoons all-purpose flour

Chocolate crème pâtissière

This is a variation on the classic crème pâtissière on page 105. Try it as an alternative base for Fruit Tartlets (page 105), as a filling for Millefeuilles (page 171) or Éclairs (page 188), or to make your own experiments.

Put the milk into a heavy-based saucepan. Using a sharp knife, split the vanilla bean along its length, scrape the seeds into the milk, then put the pod halves in too. Add half of the sugar and the cocoa powder.

Put the egg yolks and the remaining sugar into a bowl and whisk until pale and creamy. Add the flour and mix until smooth.

Put the pan of milk over medium heat, bring to just under a boil, then slowly pour half of it into the egg mixture, whisking well as you do so. Add the remainder of the milk and whisk again, then pour the mixture back into the pan. Bring

to a boil, whisking all the time, then keep boiling and whisking continuously for 1 minute. Remove from the heat.

Pour the mixture into a clean bowl and scoop out the vanilla pods. (You can wash and dry them and keep them in a jar of sugar, which will give you vanilla-flavored sugar for use in all your baking.) Cover the surface of the crème pâtissière with parchment paper straightaway to prevent a skin forming. Allow to cool, then store in the refrigerator until you're ready to use it.

Makes about 1⅔ cups

1 cup whole milk

1 heaping tablespoon good-quality ground coffee

3 egg yolks

4½ tablespoons superfine sugar

3½ tablespoons all-purpose flour

Coffee crème pâtissière

You could use this version of crème pâtissière to fill Éclairs (page 188) or Chouquettes (page 192).

Put the milk and coffee into a heavy-based saucepan.

Put the egg yolks and sugar into a bowl and whisk until pale and creamy. Add the flour and mix until smooth.

Put the pan of milk and coffee over medium heat and bring to just under a boil. Remove from the heat and pass through a fine sieve into a measuring cup or bowl, then slowly add half of it to the egg mixture, whisking well as you do so. Add the remainder of the milk and whisk again, then pour the mixture back into the pan. Bring to a boil, whisking all the time, then keep boiling and whisking continuously for 1 minute. Remove from the heat.

Pour the mixture into a clean bowl and cover the surface of the crème pâtissière with parchment paper straightaway to prevent a skin forming. Allow to cool, then store in the refrigerator until you're ready to use it.

Makes about 1¼ cups

1 cup whole milk

½ vanilla bean

3 egg yolks

3½ tablespoons superfine sugar

Crème anglaise

This is "English" custard (made without flour) that can be used as an accompaniment, hot or cold, to a warm tart. If you can make crème anglaise, you are halfway to making vanilla ice cream. So if you don't need all of the custard, you can churn it in an ice-cream maker.

Put the milk into a heavy-based saucepan. Using a sharp knife, split the vanilla bean along its length, scrape the seeds into the milk, then put half of the pod in too. Place over medium heat and bring to just under a boil.

Put the egg yolks and sugar into a bowl and whisk until pale and creamy. Slowly pour the milk into the egg mixture, whisking well as you do so. Return the mixture to the pan and place over medium heat. Using a wooden spoon, stir continuously in a figure eight until the custard thickens enough to coat the back of the spoon. (To test, lift the spoon out of the custard and draw a line down the back of the spoon with your finger. If the line stays clean, the custard is ready.) Strain immediately into a clean bowl and continue stirring for a few minutes. (You can wash and dry the halved vanilla pod and keep it in a jar of sugar, along with the unused half of the pod, which will give you vanilla-flavored sugar for use in all your baking.)

Serve hot, or leave to cool, then store in the refrigerator, covered with plastic wrap, until you're ready to use it.

Makes about 1⅔ cups

¾ cup plus 2 tablespoons whole milk

1 vanilla bean

2 egg yolks

4½ tablespoons sugar

3 tablespoons all-purpose flour

7 tablespoons heavy cream

Crème légère

This is a beautiful, classical cream that is halfway between crème pâtissière and chantilly cream. I call it an "ambient ice cream," which is, of course, a contradiction in terms, but it has all the flavor of a great vanilla ice cream without being frozen. You make the base in the same way as crème patissière, let it become cold, then whisk in some heavy cream so that you end up with something that is less dense than crème pâtissière, but more substantial than chantilly cream. It is also a fantastic way of stretching some crème pâtissière that you have left over. Use it instead of crème pâtissière as a base for fruit tarts or tartlets (see pages 105), in Millefeuilles (page 171) or Chouquettes (page 192), or substitute it for the chantilly cream to make swans' feathers (see page 181). It is also perfect for dipping strawberries into. A big bowl of berries, a bowl of crème légère, some little Shortbread (page 143) or Langues de Chat (page 147) cookies, and a glass of dessert wine at the end of a summer evening: beautiful!

Put the milk into a heavy-based saucepan. Using a sharp knife, split the vanilla bean along its length, scrape the seeds into the milk, then put the pod halves in, too.

Put the egg yolks and sugar into a bowl and whisk until pale and creamy. Add the flour and mix until smooth.

Put the pan of milk over medium heat, bring to just under a boil, then slowly pour half of it into the egg mixture, whisking well as you do so. Add the remainder of the milk and whisk again, then pour the mixture back into the pan. Bring to a boil, whisking all the time, then keep boiling and whisking continuously for 1 minute. Remove from the heat.

Pour the mixture into a clean bowl and scoop out the vanilla pods. (You can wash and dry the pods and keep them in a jar of sugar, which will give you vanilla-flavored sugar for use in all your baking.) Cover the surface of the mixture with parchment paper straightaway to prevent a skin forming. Allow to cool, then store in the refrigerator until cold and you're ready to use it.

Whisk the cream until thick and fluffy. Whisk the cold base mixture, then mix in the cream with a wooden spoon.

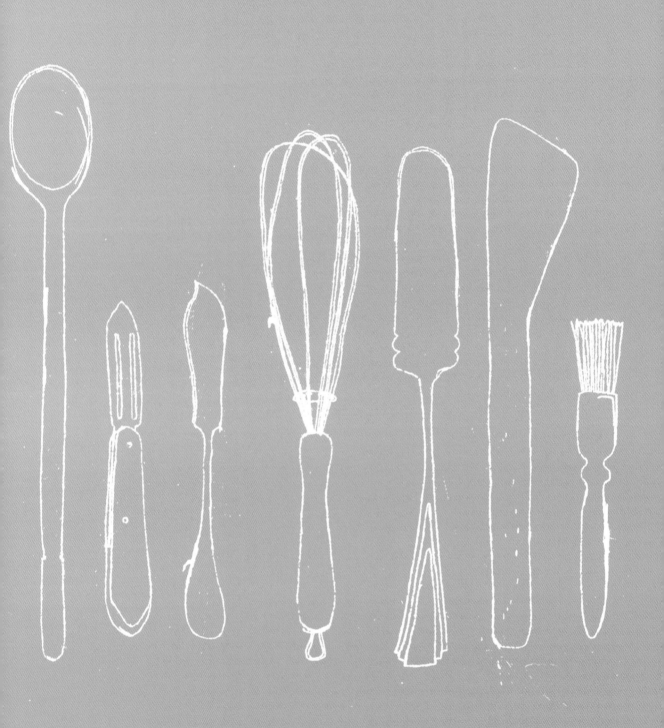

Bertinet Online

For bowls, rolling pins, whisks, pastry brushes, cooling racks, tins, cutters, and pans seen in this book, we have a selection at The Bertinet Kitchen:

The Bertinet Kitchen
12 St Andrew's Terrace
Bath, BA1 2QR
UK
www.thebertinetkitchen.com

To hone your pastry skills and watch videos of Richard making the sweet, puff, and choux pastries, visit his website at:

www.bertinetkitchen.com/videos

You can also watch Richard use the sweet pastry to make a fruit tart (a large version of the Fruit Tartlets recipe on page 105) and the choux pastry to make Swans (page 181).

And to follow the steps in the book for making the pastries as Richard talks you through them, turn to the relevant sections:

Salted and Sweet: pages 16–27

Puff: pages 44–55

Choux: pages 56–61

Index

G

galette des rois 165–67
glazes
    apricot 205
    chocolate 188–89
    egg 40
    poaching syrup glaze 122–25

H

hazelnut and almond pastry 17
hot-water crust pastry 85–97

I

Italian cookies 144–45

J

jelly
    for duck pie 80–83
    for pork pies 85, 96, 98–99
    traditional pork pie 98–99

K

kiwis, presentation tips 204

L

langues de chat 146–47
leek, reblochon, and bacon tartlets 68
lemon
    cheesecakes 116–17
    langues de chat 146–7
    meringue tartlets 113–15
    pastry 17
    tartlets 108–9

M

mascarpone cheesecakes 116–17
measures 12
meringue tartlets, lemon 113–15
millefeuilles 170–71
mince pies, frangipane 136–37
mushroom
    savory slices 150–51
    and spinach tartlets 68

N

natas (Portuguese custard tarts) 172–73

O

onion tartlets 71
open tart (savory) 72–73
orange
    and chocolate cookies 141
    langues de chat 146–47
    presentation tips 204
oven thermometers 13
ovens 13, 37

P

palmiers 174–75
parsley and smoked salmon tart 68
passion fruit cheesecakes 116–17
pasties, Cornish 16, 78–79
peach and rosemary almond tarts
    122–25
pear Bourdaloue 126–27
pies
    duck 80–83
    frangipane mince 136–37
    pork 84–99
piping bag techniques 61, 181–83, 188
pistachio
    croustillants 176–77

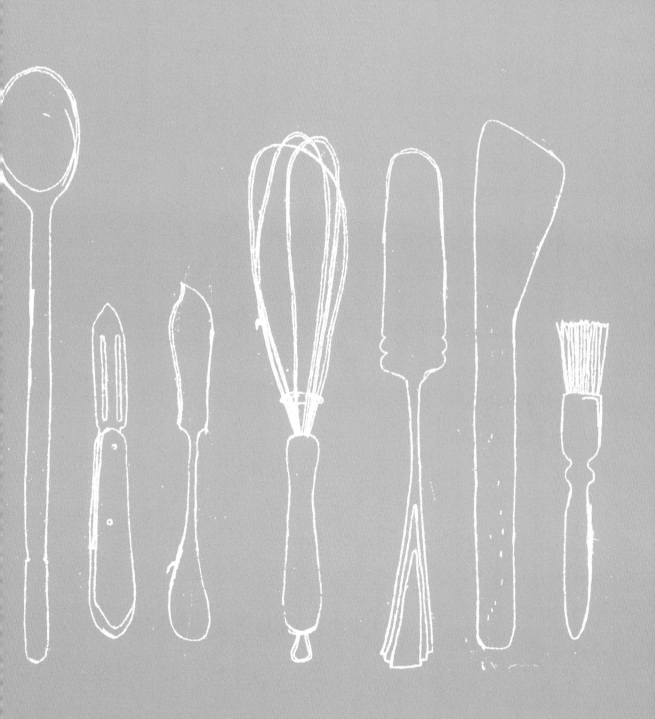

Acknowledgments

This book has been written amidst a year of change and development for our business. I am hugely indebted to the whole team, particularly Debbie, Carrie, and Sarah, and my bakers Kieron, Brett, John, Mark, and Will, who make many of the pastries in this book daily.

A huge thank-you to Sheila Keating for her unfailing ability to transform my words into wonderfully readable text; to Imogen for her drive and vision to give this book a home; to Carey, Sarah, Ed, Katie, Rae, Alice, and all at Ebury for their support and for "getting it"; to Jean Cazals for the beautiful photographs—surely another award for you within these pages, Jean! To Will for the design and layout; Trish Burgess for her copyediting; Charlotte for her fantastic drawings and lovely handwriting; and to Jess for her work on the recipes and during the shoots. Finally, thank-you to Jo—my rock and the best friend, wife, and mother to my brood I could wish for, without whom the show would not stay on the road.